CONTENTS

SECTION I
HOW TO READ REVELATION

SECTION II
THE OPENING VISION

SECTION III
THE SEVEN LETTERS

SECTION IV
PREPARATION FOR OPENING
THE SCROLL

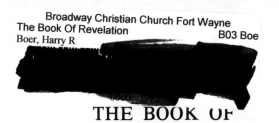

THE BOOK OF

REVELATION

by

HARRY R. BOER

Formerly Principal of the
Theological College of Northern Nigeria

WILLIAM B. EERDMANS PUBLISHING COMPANY
GRAND RAPIDS, MICHIGAN

© AFRICA CHRISTIAN PRESS

First published 1979
by Africa Christian Press
P.O. Box 30, Achimota, Ghana

First USA edition 1979
by William B. Eerdmans Publishing Company
Grand Rapids, Michigan

Library of Congress Cataloging in Publication Data

Boer, Harry R.
   The book of Revelation.

    1. Bible. N. T. Revelation—Commentaries.
I. Title.
BS2825.3.B54   1978   228'.07   78-15447
ISBN 0-8028-1748-3

SECTION X
THE SEVEN BOWLS OF GOD'S WRATH

SECTION XI
THE HARLOT AND THE BEAST

SECTION XII
THE REWARD OF THE MARTYRS AND
THE FINAL JUDGMENT

SECTION XIII
THE ETERNAL CITY

FOREWORD

THE PURPOSE of these studies is simple. It is hoped that they will help those who read them to understand and apply to their lives more of the great riches of wisdom and knowledge that the Scriptures contain. Such studies cannot hope to cover every detail of each verse. They make an attempt to consider the main points of teaching in a passage. The purpose is not just that these studies should feed the mind with the knowledge of Scripture and its teaching. Each section ends with a part entitled *Meaning for Today*, because the reading of the Bible should always lead us to the response of repentance and faith and obedience, and we express this in prayer and in action in our daily lives.

The Revised Standard Version is the translation which has been used, because of the greater simplicity of its English, and because of the increasing use of this version in places where this book may be read.

HOW TO READ REVELATION

The study of Revelation, like setting out on an expedition
of discovery, should not be undertaken without some preparation. Those who have explored the book before us
have made many helpful discoveries which can make our
study of it both easier and more fruitful. Such helps are,
in fact, so necessary that without them even the most
careful study will not lead to proper understanding.
Between the writing of Revelation and our reading of it
lie nineteen centuries of change in history, language,
religious ideas, and culture. This is a barrier too high and
wide to leap over without help. To the question, 'Do you
understand what you are reading?' one can only reply,
'How can I unless someone guides me?' (Acts 8:30,31).
The barriers can be bridged. The Church has never
stopped studying Revelation. Every generation through
study and experience has contributed to its understanding. Through these efforts Christ has fulfilled His
promise that His Spirit would lead the Church into the
truth. To study Revelation without using the insights that
the past has given to us would be an act of pride and
ingratitude.

1 The Church and the Roman empire

When John wrote at the end of the first century, eight
hundred and fifty years had already passed since the
founding of Rome. The great empire was now at the height
of its power. Eighty of its most splendid years under the
emperors Trajan, Hadrian, Antoninus Pius, and Marcus
Aurelius were about to begin.

The Church on the other hand, was still in its infancy.
For the first thirty years of its life Rome had been favour-
ably disposed to it. Judaism was a recognized religion,

and to most Romans Christianity was simply a Jewish sect (Acts 18:12). In the reign of the emperor Nero, 54-68, the distinction between Judaism and Christianity became plain. It began to be regarded as *religio illicita* (unauthorized religion), and this was to remain so until the fourth century when the emperor Constantine, 306-337, gave it official status. The severe persecutions in Rome under Nero in 64 and in other parts of the empire under Domitian in 95 were forerunners of the great trials that were to come. John suffered exile on Patmos under Domitian. In the course of it he received the visions that revealed the dark future of the Church as also the glory of her final victory. Chapters 12, 13, 14, 17, and 18 make clear what was not expressly stated in the earlier chapters, namely that Rome would oppose the Church with a power that only Christ could overcome.

2 The unity and scope of Revelation

The extent of John's vision, however, stretches far beyond the Roman empire and the Church of his time. In Revelation the Roman empire is a symbol of the opposition of the world to the Church of Christ. The churches to which he wrote represented in their varying conditions the worldwide Church in all the history of her existence. John pictures the conflict between the two at its deepest levels. Herein lie both the unity and the scope of Revelation. The New Testament calls the period between the first and the second coming of Christ the time of the End. It is in this period of time that the conflict which John describes takes place. Revelation is therefore a study in eschatology (from the Greek words *eschatos* = end, and *logos* = word, account). It is a report about the End-time. As such, the book is a vast and majestic view of things to come. It reveals the weakness of mighty empires, the poverty of wealthy nations, the feebleness and power of the Church. It shows the cosmic Christ, his arch-enemy the dragon Satan, and the allies of both in heaven, in hell, and on the earth. It pictures their armies meeting in mighty battle, and it concludes with the destruction of evil, the establishing of the good, and the revelation of the new heavens and the new earth.

Nevertheless, what is revealed here in only part of the Church's and the world's history. Both of them have large histories in other and quite different areas. These other areas Revelation does not describe or discuss. It says very little about the missionary outreach and victories of the Church, its varied service to men, and its ever deepening knowledge of the Word of God. It does not dwell on the quiet and peaceful lives that thousands of her members have been privileged to lead, and the happiness of the Christian home. The development of Christian culture in music, literature, and art, the stimulus it has given to liberation from bondage and to the banishing of ignorance, are not considered. There is no appreciation in Revelation for Paul's high estimate of the powers of government in Romans 13:1-7. It says nothing about the frequently happy relations between Church and State, and very little about the progress of society in medicine, in the economy, and in the sciences.

This is not a criticism of Revelation. It is intended rather to emphasize the strictly limited scope of the book. This is to show that, in the end, all aspects of life that are not subject to God stand in opposition to Him. It aims to show that both divine and satanic powers take part in the conflict between the Church and the world. It presents the victory of Christ and His saints in the great struggle, and it discloses the resulting order of life in a new heaven and a new earth in which righteousness will dwell.

3   The plan of the book

Without a fairly clear idea of how one part is related to the other parts, the unity of the whole is lost and the visions that John saw become meaningless. The message of Revelation is basically simple and the structure of the book is basically simple too. Revelation, like a good speech, has three parts: an Introduction, a Body, and a Conclusion.

The Introduction consists of John's opening vision and seven letters to seven churches. This covers chapters 1 to 3.

The Body consists of three groups of judgments. They cover chapters 4 to 16. Many of these judgments fall on all men, believers and unbelievers alike. For unbelievers they are a punishment and a call to repentance. For believers they are a testing and a strengthening of faith. Each group consists of seven judgments. They are presented in the form of seven seals, seven trumpets, and seven bowls of the wrath of God. These three groups are closely related to each other. The judgments of the second group flow out of the last judgment of the first group, and the judgments of the third group flow out of the last judgment of the second.

Suffering always carries the temptation to question God's faithfulness, love, and goodness. All three groups are therefore preceded by a section that may be called a preparation against such temptation. Like the world, believers suffer from the judgments of God against the sin of man; unlike the world, this suffering does not lead them to harden their hearts, but to deepen their trust and patience.

Between the second and third groups of judgment there is a most important interruption. It consists of chapters 12, 13, and 14. These three chapters are introduced at this point to reveal the spiritual background to the struggle between the Church and the world. Here the great antagonists are disclosed. On the one hand are the woman clothed with the sun, and her son Christ. Over against them stand the dragon, the beast, the false prophet, and the Babylon-like harlot.

The Conclusion consists of chapters 17 to 22. They show the final judgment on the forces that opposed God and oppressed the Church. They show the victory of Christ, the reward of the saints, and the glorious beginning of the new heaven and the new earth which shall abide for ever.

4   The nature of apocalyptic writing

Revelation belongs to that body of sacred Jewish writings described as apocalyptic. In the Bible and in Jewish literature as a whole there are various types of writing: historical (such as Samuel), prophetic (Isaiah), poetic (Psalms), wisdom (Proverbs), letter (Philippians), and apocalyptic (Daniel). Revelation belongs to this last class of literature. A large body of apocalyptic writing was produced in the two centuries B.C. and in the first century A.D. To us Revelation seems a strange, mysterious, peculiar kind of book. We cannot associate it with the kinds of writing to which we are accustomed. There was no well-informed Jew who could say such a thing in A.D. 100. Not only was it a well-known kind of writing, it was also very popular.

The word 'apocalyptic' comes from the Greek word *apokalupsis*, which in turn is related to the verb *apokalupto*, which means 'I uncover, I reveal, I disclose'. The noun form *apokalupsis* accordingly means revelation, disclosure. It is the very first word of the book in the Greek version. Apocalyptic literature is therefore revelation literature. What does it reveal? The characteristics of both biblical and extra-biblical apocalyptic writing are the same. The following are the main features of apocalyptic writing:

a. In it the universe is divided into two camps: that of the good and that of the evil. This good and evil are not simply forces and powers, but *personal* forces and powers. In Revelation the good forces are God, the World Ruler, and Christ, who is called the Lamb and the Rider on the white horse. The evil forces are the dragon (Satan) and his two servants—the beast (the emperor-worshipping state) and the false prophet (the political and religious power of such a state). Below these are such lesser powers as angels and demons, good men and evil men. These two camps are engaged in a long and fearful struggle. The great supernatural powers in these two camps work among men, in the struggles of society and in the Church. They affect nature and the history of nations. In everyday life it is not easy to distinguish the works of the two clearly, but in the end every human being is found to be on the one side or the other. The final separation between the two is the meaning of judgment.

b. Apocalyptic literature is concerned with eschatology. Revelation presents its picture of the End-time in a distinctive New Testament manner. When the New Testament speaks of the End, it does not have in mind simply the period of time immediately preceding the final judgment. In the New Testament, as already noted, the End is that period of time between the first and the second coming of Christ. The birth of Jesus introduced the End. That is why Jesus could say, 'the hour is coming, *and now is*, when the dead will hear the voice of the Son of God, and those who hear will live' (John 5:25). Revelation is therefore concerned with 'what must soon take place' (1:1). This 'soon' is not clock time or calendar time; it is End-time, God's time. The drama that unfolds in Revelation is now taking place. One of the benefits of reading

13

Revelation is to be sharpened in our awareness of this great fact.

c.   Visions and symbols are characteristic of all apocalyptic writing. So great and majestic are the visions of the apocalyptic writers that they are unable to describe them in the language of everyday life. They write in such a manner that the reader seems to understand what is written by feeling it rather than by intellectually grasping it. Just as laughter, tears, a handshake, silence, gestures, often say things that words cannot express, so the visions of apocalyptic writing say more than words can carry. Symbolic language leads the reader to make pictures in his own mind of things and ideas that are too deep, too emotionally heavy, to express in words of common speech.

The symbolic language is sometimes John's own. More often it is drawn from two other sources. These are the Old Testament and the Apocrypha. Although Daniel is the only truly apocalyptic book in the Old Testament, there is apocalyptic language and scenery in a number of other Old Testament books, notably in Ezekiel. John also used ordinary language and figures in an apocalyptic manner, such as throne, temple, altar, angels, numbers, precious stones, animal forms. The Apocrypha are Jewish religious writings which were not a part of the Hebrew Old Testament. The word 'apocrypha' comes from a Greek word meaning 'to be hidden'. It was a sort of special writing meant only for those who could understand it. From these three sources, then, his own imaginative thought, the Old Testament, and the Apocrypha, John drew the symbols, the language, the imagery that makes Revelation the book that it is. But let it not be forgotten that Revelation is *revelation*. Behind all the explainable factors, data, and backgrounds stands the inspiring Holy Spirit, who revealed to John the mysterious and deep things of God.

d.   The meaning of John's language can usually be determined from the manner in which his images are used in the Old Testament or in the Apocrypha. Sometimes the reader must supply the meaning himself. But whether he finds the meaning or supplies the meaning, he must be prepared to read imaginatively. He must learn to live in a world of strange animal forms, insects with human qualities, roaring waterfalls, burning stars falling from the

14

sky, smoking pits from which millions of locusts fly forth, a mighty angel placing one foot on a continent, another in the ocean, and hailstones that weigh more than a hundred pounds.

Through such forms, pictures, shapes, figures, symbols, John speaks his message concerning the struggle between light and darkness, life and death, good and evil, the Church and the world, Christ and Satan. In it all, and in a manner never equalled before or after, he proclaims God's cosmic judgment and salvation in the time of the *eschatos*, the End-time.

5 The history of interpretation

It will not surprise us to learn that a book of such a nature has been interpreted in various ways. These interpretations have often been deeply influenced by the relationship of the Church to the world around it in different periods of its history. Some viewpoints that were once held widely have been abandoned altogether. Other interpretations are as alive today as centuries ago when they were first proposed. The reading of Revelation will be more rewarding when we have a general view of the various ways in which the book has been understood in the past. The following major interpretations should be noted.

a. From 150 to 250

About the middle of the second century Justin Martyr, one of the first apologists of Christianity in the Roman world, gave a significant interpretation of Revelation. For him and for many others of his time the most important teaching of the book centred around the thousand years' reign of Christ as presented in chapter 20. At His coming Christ would destroy Rome (the Babylon of Revelation) and its emperor the Anti-Christ. Thereupon He would establish His thousand years' reign. At the end of the thousand years the resurrection and the judgement would bring an end to human history. The thousand years' kingdom was expected to come in the more or less near future. The latest expected date for its beginning was around the year five hundred. Today Justin Martyr's view would be called premillennial. This is the teaching that the coming of Christ will take place before (*pre*) the introduction of the millennium (from the Latin *mille* = thousand, *annus* = year).

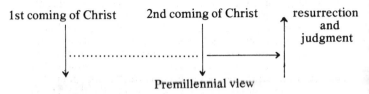

1st coming of Christ   2nd coming of Christ   resurrection and judgment

Premillennial view

Another important reading of Revelation was proposed by Hippolytus, a Roman theologian who died in 235. He considered that the three series of judgments (the seven seals, the seven trumpets, and the seven bowls of the wrath of God) that dominate chapters 4 to 16 do not follow each other. Rather, they are to be seen as different descriptions of the same period of time, namely from the first coming of Christ to the second. With different visions and symbols the second and third series repeat the first. This view is held by many interpreters today.

b. From 250 to 400
In this period a new emphasis arose which was quite different from that of Justin Martyr or Hippolytus. It was an interpretation that was not historical but allegorical or figurative. The seven heads of the dragon are not kings or emperors but represent the seven deadly sins. The scroll with seven seals is the Bible, which Christ alone can explain. There will be a conflict between Christ and Anti-Christ, but it will be a spiritual conflict. The future is left unclear. The chief theologian of this view was Origen of Alexandria, who died in 254. Few interpreters have adopted this approach to the book. Its importance lies in the fact that to some extent and in one form or another allegorism plays a role in all forms of interpretation.

c. From 400 to 1500
In about 390, Tychonius, a leader in the North African Donatist church, proposed an interpretation that has remained influential to the present day. He taught that the thousand years of Revelation 20 are not to be seen as a future period of time, but as the period extending from the

first coming of Christ to the second. That is to say, the millennium is now. Augustine adopted this view and gave the prestige of his name to it. By His death and resurrection Christ has bound Satan, the strong man (Matthew 12:29), and is now claiming His possessions for God's kingdom. Augustine had been a premillennialist, but when the premillennialist interpretation began to become ridiculous because of its exaggerations, he adopted the view of Tychonius. For eleven centuries it has been the dominant view in the Church. It is generally known as amillennialism (from *a* = no, + millennium). What this means is that according to the Augustinian view there is no millennium at all in the premillennial sense of the word.

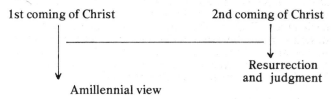

1st coming of Christ   2nd coming of Christ

Resurrection and judgment

Amillennial view

Another view which has also had many followers is the view that the second and third groups of judgments in chapters 4 to 16 do not repeat the first group (as in the view of Hippolytus), but that the one follows the other. They represent stages in the history of the Church.

d. From 1500 to the present

The Reformation took place in the first half of the sixteenth century. With it began a long period of hostility and criticism between Catholics and Protestants. Already in the time before the Reformation the Pope had been viewed as the Anti-Christ prophesied in Revelation. With the Reformation this tendency became stronger. Catholic scholars denied the possibility of identifying the Pope with the Anti-Christ of Revelation. They did so by viewing Revelation as a book that spoke to its own time, when as yet there was no Pope. The leading writer in this movement was the Spanish Jesuit, Alcasar, who published a commentary on Revelation in 1614. He divided his book into four parts: chapters 1 to 4 of Revelation were presented as the introductory part; chapters 5 to 11 as a conflict between the Church and Judaism; chapters 12 to 19 as the conflict between the Church and the Roman empire; and chapters 20 to 22 as the victory of the Church over her enemies. The millennium begins with emperor Constantine, who bound Satan and made the empire Christian. Since the 'Anti-Christ in Revelation is a premillennial figure it is not possible that he should represent the Pope. From the time of Constantine on to shortly before the return of Christ, the Anti-Christ lies bound in the bottomless pit (Revelation 20:1-3). There is perhaps no clearer example of a historical situation influencing the interpretation of Revelation.

During this period another view developed which was influential for a while but has since had little support. It is called postmillennialism (from *post* = after, plus millennium). It holds that as a result of the gospel and the Christian presence in the world, there will be a gradual progress toward a society obedient to God. Such a society will be the millennium. Jesus will return after this millennium has run its course. The history of the twentieth century with its many destructive events has not encouraged the hope that the society of man will develop in any such way as postmillennialism envisages.

As one reads the history of the interpretation of Revelation, one is overwhelmingly impressed with the Europe-centred character of it. When Americans write about Revelation, they do not do so as a new force or with a new vision, but simply as an extension of Europe. Africa and Asia do not come into the picture. The thought that Europe might cease to be the centre of the Christian world, or cease to be even a centre at all (such as happened in the Middle East and North Africa), never seriously entered the minds of Western commentators. Still less have Africa and Asia been seen as world areas in which the Church might find large and rich, perhaps its fullest expression. Revelation has indeed been deeply studied by the Western Church. No interpretation of it can possibly afford to ignore the thought given to the Apocalypse by the Western theological mind. But neither may any interpretation of it be considered to be final. The entire Church, throughout the ages, must bend its mind to the understanding of Revelation. The time has more than come for Africa and Asia to take up the task.

6 The purpose of Revelation
Revelation was written to show God's servants 'what must soon take place' (1:1). The End-time, in which the events pictured in the book will happen, will be a time of suffering for the Church, of testing of its faith, and of revelation of the power and grace of God. Faithfulness in suffering to the end will be rewarded by a manifestation of inexpressible glory. The message that God gave to John is therefore one that prepares the Church for what is coming upon it; that message will comfort the Church in its trials and hold before it the glory that is to follow. The basis of all warning, encouragement, comfort, and hope is that the victory has already been won. For this reason there can be a constant lifting of the curtain to reveal the power, the majesty, and the joy in the heavenly throne-room, and the victory that is already being celebrated there.

7 Authorship and date
Revelation was written by an author named John. From early times he was understood to be the apostle John. This was the view of ancient authorities like Justin Martyr, Irenaeus, Tertullian, and Origen. Papias, one of the apostolic fathers living in the first half of the second century, writes in such a way that an elder named John may be distinguished from the apostle John. Some consider this John to be 'the elder' (2 John 1:1, 3 John 1:1) who wrote the second and third Johannine letters. Others believe that still a third John named John the Seer is the author of Revelation. In the absence of more positive evidence it is reasonable to incline to the view that John the apostle wrote the book. As a matter of considered judgment, however, the question of authorship is best left open.

About the date of writing, too, there are varying views. The main schools of thought hold that it was written either at the end of Nero's reign in 68 or toward the end of the reign of Domitian around 95. The latter view is favoured by most students of the book. One reason is that the spiritual condition of some of the churches to which John wrote requires the later date. They reveal a spiritual poverty which, it is believed, took a longer time to develop than the earlier date permits. John's exile, as far distant from Rome as Patmos (near Asia Minor), would also fit better into A.D. 95 than 64. It indicates a broader persecution than the one under Nero, which appears to have been confined to Rome.

8 Form of writing

Though it may not seem so to us, Revelation is really not a book but a letter. It is a rather unusual sort of letter, but it is in fact a letter. When we compare its salutation to the churches (1:4-8) and the conclusion (22:6-21) with the salutations and conclusions of the letters of Paul, 1 Peter, and 3 John, this will become plain. Between the opening salutation and the closing benediction lie twenty-two chapters, twenty of which are apocalyptic writing. The non-apocalyptic chapters, 2 and 3, are letters within the letter. The apocalyptic material could not be put into typical letter form. Nevertheless, John used the accepted way of letter writing to tell the churches the things that must shortly come to pass. When an engineer, a scientist, or a doctor writes a long professional letter to a colleague, its message, apart from personal greeting and conclusion, cannot have much similarity to the usual type of letter. It is in some such way that the letter-form of John's prophetic-apocalyptic message must be understood. It is well to remember in this connection that John's apocalyptic imagery did not strike his readers as strange. On the contrary, it was a widely known and understood form of religious thought in the Jewish world.

THE OPENING VISION

Chapter 1

Revelation takes its name, as we have seen, from the first word of its first verse, namely revelation. To this the early Church added the words, 'of John' or 'to John'. For this there is explicit ground in 1:1.

1   Origin of the Revelation, verses 1-3

The origin of the revelation given to John is God, the Creator and Redeemer. He stands at every crucial turn in the account, such as 1:8, 4:8, 7:11, 8:2, 10:7, 19:1-6. Jesus Christ appears with Him as the Executor of God's plan (1:12-18, 6:1, 7:10, 11:15-16, 14:1, 22:1). He gives to John the revelation that God has given to Him. This is characteristic of Jesus' teaching—He has nothing of Himself, all is from His Father and He, Jesus, reveals it to men (Matthew 11:27, John 7:16,17, 12:49,50). Jesus sends an angel to reveal the message to John, who in turn is told to disclose it to the churches. In 22:8-16 the angel and Jesus are presented as being one and the same. It is possible to read the same identification in the first chapter (cf. verses 1,17,18).

The revelation that is given in this way is called a prophecy. It performs the two services rendered by prophecy: it instructs, admonishes, and comforts according to the will of God, and it foretells things that are to happen. Revelation is therefore a prophetic as well as an apocalyptic book of the Bible.

A blessing is pronounced on all who read, hear, and keep what is written in the prophecy. In the absence of printed Scriptures, great emphasis was laid on the public reading of the handwritten Scriptures in the early Church. Colossians 4:16, 1 Thessalonians 5:27, and Revelation 22: 7,10,18 repeat the instruction that the prophecy be publicly read, listened to, and obeyed. The reason for this is that 'the time is near'. That nearly 2,000 years have gone by since these words were written does not remove their seriousness. With God one day is as a thousand years and a thousand years as one day (2 Peter 3:8ff). The fact remains that God can today, as then, bring human history to an end. If that is so, we should live our lives in the light of the End.

2 Greetings to the seven churches, verses 4-8

John greets 'the seven churches that are in Asia'. Asia was the name of a Roman province which is today the western part of Asiatic Turkey. According to verse 11, the seven churches in question were Ephesus, Smyrna, Pergamum, Thyatira, Sardis, Philadelphia, and Laodicea. Actually, there were at least three other churches in Asia at the time of Paul, some thirty-five years earlier than John's writing. They were Troas (Acts 20:5), Hierapolis (Colossians 4:13), and Colossae, to which Paul addressed a letter. Perhaps already in John's time there were two other churches in the cities of Tralles and Magnesia. In A.D. 113 Ignatius, bishop of Antioch in Syria, sent letters to them. It would appear therefore that John chose to write to seven rather than to all the churches in Asia Minor. This probably had a symbolic purpose, the number seven representing the Church in its completeness.

John pronounces a benediction on the churches in a form found nowhere else in the New Testament. Grace and peace are extended from 'him who is and who was and who is to come'. The context makes clear that this refers to God the Father. It may therefore seem that it would have been more appropriate to use the designation 'him who is and who was and who shall be'. But John writes, 'who is to come'. The expression is also used in 1:8 and 4:8. In 22:12, 13 Jesus identifies Himself as the coming one. He also takes the name Alpha and Omega by which the Father designates Himself in 1:8. There is therefore a very close connection between the Father and the Son. This is part of the New Testament data for the doctrine of the Trinity.

Grace and peace are also given from the 'seven spirits that are before his throne'. In Revelation the number 7 is a highly significant figure. The book is full of symbols, and numbers and fractions of numbers are an inseparable part of the symbolism. Three, four, five, seven, ten, twelve, a half, a third, a fourth, large numbers in the thousands, and the mysterious number 666 (13:18) are basic elements in the picture language of the book. Of all these, however, seven is the most used and the most important. It is used symbolically scores of times in the Bible. It is probably derived from a similar symbolic use in the Semitic world in which Israel lived. For reasons that can no longer be determined, the number seven came to symbolize fulness, completeness, perfection. The seven spirits before God's throne represents therefore the fulness of the Holy Spirit. (See also 3:1, 4:5, 5:6.)

Grace and peace are given to the churches 'from Jesus Christ, the faithful witness, the first-born of the dead, and the ruler of kings on earth'. The faithfulness of Jesus' witness was complete, even to death. It was followed by His resurrection and the receiving of all authority in heaven and on earth (Matthew 28:18). As crucified and risen, He knows the depths of humiliation and the heights of glory. To Him John dedicates a magnificent doxology (5-6). He then strongly emphasizes that Jesus is the coming one. With a final statement from the Lord God that He is the Beginning and the End (Alpha and Omega are the first and last letters of the Greek alphabet), the introductory paragraphs come to a close.

3 The vision of Christ among the churches, verses 9-20
With these verses the visions of Revelation begin. When they came to him, John was on Patmos, a small island lying about forty miles southwest of Miletus in Asia Minor. It is about ten miles long, six miles wide, hilly, and was used by the Roman government as a place of banishment for political prisoners. To this island, John had been exiled. He writes that he was on Patmos 'on account of the Word of God and the testimony of Jesus', sharing with other Christians in 'the tribulation and the kingdom and the patient endurance'.

On that island and under these circumstances he was 'in the Spirit' on a Lord's day, i.e. on a Sunday. What it means to be 'in the Spirit' is described in various ways in the Bible. In his great vision, chapter 6, Isaiah simply says that he 'saw the Lord sitting upon a throne', etc. Of Ezekiel it is said that the word of the Lord came to him and 'the hand of the Lord was upon him there' (1:1). What Daniel saw he described as 'dreams and visions of his head', and 'night visions' (7:1,2,7,13). Peter in Acts 10:10 was 'in a trance' and saw heaven opened. Vision is like the dream condition but is not the same. The prophet keeps his consciousness but is lifted out of his normal waking state. The vision may come to him at night or during waking hours. In the Bible, vision is a means of revelation. It is a way in which the Word of God may come to a prophet. The entire prophecy of Isaiah is called a vision (1:1), as is also that of Amos (1:1). The book of Obadiah is called 'the vision of Obadiah', although there is no vision in the usual sense of the word in it. The vision of Obadiah is 'Thus says the Lord God concerning Edom' (1:1). A vision may therefore be described as an avenue of divine revelation. In its usual form something is shown in a dramatic or symbolic manner that is not visible to ordinary sight.

John says he heard a loud voice behind him 'like a trumpet'. All of John's visions are characterized by strength, power, might. Everything in that world of God that was revealed to him is immeasurably stronger, more powerful, mightier than the world in which he, John, lived. The eyes of the one who spoke to him were like a flame of fire, His voice as the sound of many waters, His tongue like a sharp two-edged sword, His face like the sun shining in full strength. The Church was weak; the Christians were few and without strength. The Roman empire that oppressed them was everywhere present and seemed irresistible. It was the beast described in chapter thirteen, so invincible that men under its power could only say, 'Who is like the beast, and who can fight against it?' The comfort and the hope that John's visions gave to him and to the Church were that the persecuted children of God live under the protection of a Power beside which the Roman empire is as nothing.

The voice speaking like a trumpet told him to write down what he saw and to send it to the seven churches, which are mentioned by name. These will be discussed as a group in the introductory part of the next chapter.

When John turned to see who spoke to him in this way, he saw seven golden lampstands. A man described as 'one like a son of man' walked among these lampstands and in His right hand He held seven stars. This is the heart, the centre, of John's first vision. All the descriptive material in verses 12-20 is intended only to strengthen and give power to this basic vision of the seven lampstands, the son of man, and the seven stars in His hand. What then is the meaning of this basic vision?

The lampstands represent seven distinct, existing churches in seven distinct, existing cities in Asia Minor. On the other hand, the number seven signifies that these churches represent the full, the universal Church of Christ. The picture of the lampstand is drawn from Zechariah 4:2, which presents a lampstand with seven lamps. John has seven stands with one lamp each. The light that they shed is the Word of God. It is a lamp for our feet, a light on our path (Psalm 119:105); Israel has been set as a light for the nations (Isaiah 42:6, 49:6); believers are the light of the world (Matthew 5:14); once they were darkness but now they are light in the Lord (Ephesians 5:8). The churches spread this light through the witness, fellowship, life, and love of their members.

The seven stars may well be the pastors or leaders of the churches. They have a special responsibility and are therefore carried in the hand of Christ, in His right hand of power. It is to be noted, however, that on the one hand John must send his book to the seven churches (verse 11); on the other hand, the letters in chapters 2 and 3 are all addressed individually to the angels of the seven churches. The angel (which here probably means pastor) appears to represent the entire congregation, and what is written to him is written to the whole of his church.

The one who walks among the churches and holds their leaders in His hand is 'one like a son of man'. This was the favourite self-designation of Jesus: Matthew 8:20, 9:6, 16:13; Mark 2:10, 8:38; Luke 5:24, 18:8; John 6:27, 12:23, and many other places. It is derived from Daniel 7:13,14. One 'like a son of man' appears there as a heavenly being in human form to whom is given glory, dominion, and power over the nations. In Jesus, Daniel's vision is fulfilled. Now He reigns unseen, but one day He will appear openly to all.

So overwhelming was the appearance of Christ that John fell as one dead before Him. But the Lord comforted him, and spoke the familiar words, 'Fear not'. He is the first and the last, the beginning and the end of both creation and redemption; by His death He has conquered death, lives for ever and ever, and has the keys of, i.e. the power over, death and the world of the dead (Hades).

A small but significant matter for the reading of Revelation as a whole is the passage, 'he laid his right hand upon me'. How could Jesus lay His right hand on John when He was holding seven stars in it? Such details never bother John. In the world of revelation by vision, up can be down and down can be up. Christ has a special concern for His Church and its leaders—that is the meaning of the stars in His right hand. Christ loves and comforts His fearful servants—that is the meaning of His right hand on John's shoulder. If you were to ask John what the Lord did with the stars while He laid his right hand on John, he would look at you in perplexity and say, 'What has that got to do with it? You don't seem to understand me'. The world of apocalyptic vision is rich, powerful, full of meaning. It does not pretend to be mathematically or logically exact. It can put two where there is room for only one; it marvellously gives scorpions' tails to locusts; hail and fire are mixed with blood; a book is eaten which gives a sweet taste in the mouth and a bitter feeling in the stomach. Revelation is full of such wonderful pictures, symbols, and figures. In all of this the question is not, 'what is the logic of the vision?' but, 'what is the meaning?' This is the principle that underlies much of traditional African and contemporary Western art, notably in the work of the late Pablo Picasso, who was deeply influenced by African art.

Meaning for today

The secret of Christian peace in a time of persecution or suffering is a vision of the unseen world of divine power that watches over God's people. John was given to see that world. He saw it as no one had ever seen it before. But he was by no means the first to whom it was revealed. Alone, asleep in the wilderness, a fugitive from the anger of his elder brother, Jacob had a vision of angels ascending and descending on a ladder reaching from earth to heaven (Genesis 28:10-17). Totally defenceless against the might of Syria's army, Elisha the prophet was protected by an unseen but invincible heavenly host (2 Kings

6:11-19). Guardian angels in heaven, said Jesus, watch over His little ones (Matthew 18:10). In His agony in the garden, Jesus knew that if He called them, twelve legions of angels would come to His aid (Matthew 26:53). The angels that released Peter from gaol (Acts 12:6-11) and the earthquake that freed Paul and Silas (Acts 16:25-34) are always powers ready to the hand of God, who has said, 'I will never leave you nor forsake you.'

It was with such an experience behind him that John could write to brethren in need of encouragement and comfort, 'I John, your brother, who share with you in Jesus the tribulation *and the kingdom* and the patient endurance, was on the island called Patmos. . . .'

The moment of trial is always a lonely one. Even when many share in it with us, the fact of loneliness remains. This is because of the common powerlessness and help-lessness to escape the suffering. It is at this point that we must see the vision of the Great Power around us and over us. This vision is faith, and faith is 'the assurance of things hoped for, the conviction of things not seen' (Hebrews 11:1). John does not record that anyone was with him when the Lord appeared to him on Patmos. Daniel, in a similar experience, did have companions. He wrote:

> And I, Daniel, alone saw the vision, for the men who were with me did not see the vision, but a great trembling fell on them, and they fled to hide themselves. (10:7)

Men and women who face firmly and calmly things that terrify others, inspire admiration but also wonderment and fear in those who behold them. Sometimes they will be asked the secret of their peace. Then, like Elisha, they may pray to God, 'O Lord, I pray thee, open his eyes that he may see', and speak to men the gospel of the victorious Christ.

Revelation invites us to come to a clearer understanding of this power that we too may learn to 'fear not, for those who are with us are more than those who are with them' (2 Kings 6:16).

THE SEVEN LETTERS

Chapters 2 and 3

Chapters 2 and 3 of Revelation are undoubtedly the most read and most preached-upon chapters of the book. They are treasures of religious writing. They encourage, comfort, and warn the Church of all times and places and in all the circumstances of her varied history. Except for a few references like the Nicolaitans, Satan's throne, and Jezebel, the letters are straightforward and can easily be read and appreciated. This chapter, therefore, will limit itself to discussing the letters in general. It will explain some difficult references in them, and will conclude with a statement of their meaning for today.

1 The Church universal

There were ten, possibly twelve, churches in Asia Minor when John wrote his book, so why did he write letters only to these particular churches? Seven is the most used and the most important of the symbolic numbers found in Revelation. It means fulness, completeness, perfection. These seven churches, although living, historical churches in John's time, represent the universal Church of Jesus Christ, and each represents some aspect that is characteristic of the Church at one time or another.

Because of their faithfulness, two churches, Smyrna and Philadelphia, receive only praise.

Because of their unfaithfulness, two churches, Sardis and Laodicea, receive only blame.

Because of their mixed faithfulness and unfaithfulness, three churches, Ephesus, Pergamum, and Thyatira, receive both praise and blame.

The letters to the seven churches call the Church in every age to examine itself to find its true condition before God and to be open at all times to what the Spirit has to say.

2 The structure of the letters

All seven letters have been composed in a remarkably similar way. Yet the content that has been poured into them is so varied that the similarity of the letters is hardly noticed in the reading. The following are the leading features which all the letters have in common:

a. All are preceded by an instruction to John: 'To the angel of the church ----- write. . . .'

b. Every letter begins with the expression: 'The words of. . . .'

c. The one who speaks the words is Jesus in every case. He is introduced to the reader by means of a significant description which is different in every letter, e.g. 'The first and the last, who died and came to life', 'him who has the seven spirits of God and the seven stars'.

d. The message of each letter begins with Jesus' words, 'I know . . . .' Five times he says, 'I know your works', once, 'I know your tribulation and your poverty', and once, 'I know where you dwell'.

e. What Jesus knows is then further set forth as a description of the character, situation, and need of the church to which the letter is addressed. It may include a complaint, 'but I have this against you', or an encouragement, 'Do not fear what you are about to suffer', or an exhortation to repent, 'Those whom I love, I reprove and chasten; so be zealous and repent'.

f. In each case there is a conclusion consisting of a promise of reward, 'To him who conquers, I will give', and a call to the church, 'He who has an ear, let him hear what the Spirit says to the churches'. In three letters the call comes first and the promise second.

3 The relationship of the letters to the book

A careful comparison of the letters to the churches with the rest of Revelation raises two questions which should be discussed. The book as a whole with the exception of chapters 2 and 3 deals consistently and overwhelmingly with the suffering of the Church in persecution and her victory over that persecution. This persecution was inflicted by the Roman empire, the earthly power which the Church was unable to escape. The basic reason for the persecution was the refusal of the Church to worship the beast (chapter 13), i.e. the Roman empire, as it was personified in the god-emperor.

Of this great struggle between the Church and the empire we seem to read nothing directly in the seven letters. On the contary, the suffering of the Church to which they refer results mainly from Jewish hostility to the gospel. Expressions like false apostles, Nicolaitans, those who say they are Jews but are not, the teaching of Balaam, the woman Jezebel, the synagogue of Satan, are all Jewish in their reference.

The second problem raised by the letters when compared with the rest of the book is the question of the kind or style of writing. Revelation is a symbolic book. Only chapters 2 and 3 do not have this character. In them only the description of Jesus at the beginning of each letter is presented in consistently symbolic language. Imagery is further used in such passages as 2:5,7,10,27; 3:4,8,12,18. Yet even those symbolic expressions do not change the basic prose in which the letters are written; much less are they apocalyptic in character.

It may be said, therefore, that the Jewish reference of the letters and their non-symbolic, non-apocalyptic style of writing distinguish the seven letters markedly from the rest of the book. How is this to be understood?

The book can be read leaving out chapters 2 and 3 and the reader would not be aware of any break. This is because the letters to the seven churches were probably written by John a number of years earlier and given a place immediately after the opening vision. They deal in considerable measure with persecution or harassment of the Church. It was therefore possible to make them a significant part of Revelation. They were harmonized in some measure with the rest of the book, and were given a place immediately after the opening vision.

4 Explanation of obscure passages

a. 2:2 'those who call themselves apostles but are not.' It appears from the New Testament that the early Church appointed preachers to serve the Church as a whole. They were travelling evangelists and were sometimes called apostles. This arose from the fact of their having a ministry for the whole Church as did the twelve apostles. Apparently Barnabas was such an apostle (Acts 14:14), as were also Andronicus and Junius (Romans

16:7). In course of time some false teachers began to claim apostleship who had not been appointed to the office and who, moreover, preached a doctrine that was not Christian. John may have had these in mind when he wrote about 'false prophets' in his first letter (4:1). Paul refers to them explicitly (2 Corinthians 11:13). John praised the Church at Ephesus because it had tested such apostles and found them to be false (2:2).

b. **2:4** 'but I have this against you, that you have abandoned the love you had at first.' Precisely what John refers to here by 'the love you had at first', it is not possible to say. It is clear that the Ephesians had continued in the Christian way and for this the writer praises them. But they apparently did not do so with the same devotion, power, and self-sacrifice that they had shown when they were first introduced to Christ. Acts 19:5,6,17-20 and 20:36-38 lend support to this understanding.

c. 'The teaching of Balaam', the prophetic teaching of 'the woman Jezebel', and 'the deep things of Satan' have the same thing in mind, namely the eating of food sacrificed to idols, and its accompanying immorality. The teaching of the Nicolaitans is not specifically identified. Some of the earliest Church fathers understood the Nicolaitans and their teachings to be the same as the others. Their view has been generally accepted to the present day, but it does remain a supposition. In Greek and Roman society the feasts at which men ate food that had been sacrificed to idols easily led to immoral conduct. The early Church took a strong stand against such practices.

d. **2:9,10** 'those who say that they are Jews but are not, but are a synagogue of Satan', and 'for ten days you will have tribulation'. The reference here is to Jews who by their opposition to the gospel denied their true character as people of God. In persecuting the Church of Christ they became a synagogue of Satan. They were not the true Israel but offspring of the devil, whose will they desired to do (John 8:44). In 3:9 the same expression recurs. That some Christians would be thrown into prison for 'ten days' indicates a short period of suffering. One commentator suggests, 'for a week or so.'

e. **2:13** 'where Satan's throne is . . . where Satan dwells.' Our knowledge of the history of Pergamum helps us to understand John's meaning at this point. There were in his day three great centres of pagan religion in the city. One was a famous altar of Zeus, pre-eminent among the Greek gods as father of the human race. A second was a temple dedicated to Asclepius, the god of healing whose symbol was a serpent. The third was a temple of Augustine in which the first god-emperor of Rome was worshipped. At Pergamum, therefore, Greek popular religion, state imperial religion, and healing in the name of a pagan god combined to make the city a centre that could only be hostile to a faithfully witnessing Church. It was probably in conflict with one or more of these that Antipas, 'my witness, my faithful one', had been killed.

f.   2:17 'To him who conquers, I will give some of the hidden manna, and I will give him a white stone, with a new name written on the stone which no one knows except him who receives it.' The manna with which God fed Israel in its desert wanderings here becomes a picture of the food with which God will reward His faithful servants. It is not visible food but spiritual, and is derived from the true bread from heaven which is Christ (John 6:25,58). A foretaste of this is found especially in the Church's celebration of holy communion. The expression 'hidden manna' doubtless comes from the manna laid up in the Holy of Holies in the tabernacle (Exodus 33:16; Hebrews 9:4).

A further reward is the gift of a new name written on a white stone which only he who receives it will understand. Its scriptural background is pre-eminently Exodus 28:17-21. In the Bible as a whole, 'name', especially as applied to God, is a means of revelation. The names of God reveal God's character. God's names are identical with His being. As applied to Christ this is expressed beautifully in Matthew 1:21, 'and you shall call his name Jesus, for he will save his people from their sins'. In the new world we shall receive names that will describe our character as it really is, and we alone shall fully understand them as only Christ fully understands His (Revelation 19:12).

Its being engraved on a white stone indicates its permanence, its precious quality, and its beauty. Observe the emphasis on the quality of preciousness in the stones mentioned in Exodus 28:17-21.

g.   2:27 'And he shall rule them with a rod of iron' will be considered in connection with 19:15, where Christ is presented as one who will rule the nations with a rod of iron.

h. 3:7 '. . . who has the key of David, who opens and no one shall shut, who shuts and no one opens.' The 'key of David' is a clear reference to Isaiah 22:22, where Eliakim is promised the authority over the king's household that had been exercised by the unworthy steward Shebna: 'I will place on his shoulders the key of the house of David; he shall open and none shall shut, and he shall shut and none shall open.' The key of the palace becomes in Revelation 3:7 a symbol of the authority of Christ, David's messianic descendant, to open and close the gates of God's kingdom. Matthew 16:19 is another notable reference to this passage. The 'open door' standing before the Philadelphians shows them as a body with missionary vision and service. 1 Corinthians 16:9 is a striking parallel passage. It is known that long after the Muslims had over-run Asia Minor, the Philadelphian church continued as a faithful witness to her Lord.

Meaning for today
The letters to the seven churches were meant to describe the Church of Christ at all times, in all places, and under all circumstances. Now one, then another, letter is more relevant to a given situation. All are needed, however, to see the Church in its entirety. Therefore the letters together constitute a call to the entire Church 'to examine yourselves to see whether you are holding to your faith. Test yourselves. Do you not realize that Jesus Christ is in you?—unless indeed you fail to meet the test' (2 Corinthians 13:5).

Therefore the call remains urgent: 'He who has an ear let him hear what the Spirit says to the churches.' This self-testing in the light of the seven letters is of additional relevance for the greater part of the Church in Africa because of its youth. The letters were written to young churches. Not one of them was fifty years old when John wrote them. In the sub-Sahara or 'black Africa' thousands of Christian congregations are less than fifty years old. The first letter, to Ephesus, carries a terrible warning. It says, 'I have this against you, that you have abandoned the love you had at first. Remember then from what you have fallen, repent and do the works you did at first. If not I will come to you and remove your lamp-stand from its place, unless you repent.' Where is the lampstand of Christ's Church in North Africa today? It has nearly disappeared. By the sixth century the Church in North Africa was large, reaching from Egypt to Morocco, famous for its great leaders: Clement of Alexandria, Origen, Athanasius, Tertullian, Cyprian, St. Augustine. As a largely expatriate Church (Roman, Greek, Spanish) it lived for itself and did not evangelize. It saw a constant stream of slaves brought across the Sahara from the Sudan, but never sent missionaries to the Sudan. It did not even evangelize the Berbers in its own neighbourhood. At last its life degenerated into ecclesiastical disunity and theological argumentation. Between 640 and 700 the Muslims established themselves on the whole of the African Mediterranean shore and gradually but surely the Christian Church died out. A similar development has more recently taken place in the West, which for so long has carried the Christian cause. It is now in many areas afflicted with what is called 'post-Christianity', a term that describes a society that has massively known, massively weighed, and massively rejected the gospel of Christ. The warning, 'I will come to you and remove your lampstand from its place', is not an empty warning.

And who in the Church of Africa can read without concern the attraction which Nicolaitanism had for the early Church? Nicolaitanism was basically a sort of religious syncretism, that is, a religion that mixes Christian and pagan elements. What this does, in effect, is to create a third religion which is neither Christian nor pagan. In Ephesus, in Pergamum, in Thyatira, this mixed religion revealed itself not alongside of, but right within the Church. Although much that has been called 'pagan' is in fact healthy traditional culture that ought to be retained, there are also elements in the pre-Christian tradition that cannot be asorbed by Christianity or recognized by it as valid. The rapid multiplication of religious groupings on the continent is to an extent a combined Christo-pagan development.

There are other connections between the seven letters and Christian life today. Everywhere there are large 'open doors' to the Church in the form of opportunities for evangelization, such as confronted the church in Philadelphia. But are we not often more concerned with the erection of imposing church edifices and with the development of elaborate church programmes than with the building of God's kingdom? Of some of these it might well be true that they are said to be alive but in fact are dead. There is a great pursuit of education, wealth, and social status which leads many to have an attitude to the gospel that is neither cold nor hot. And let not those be forgotten who live in poverty in the cities and in the rural areas but who in fact are rich in Christ. Every one of the seven churches finds its counterpart among us today, from poor-but-rich Smyrna to Laodicea that was neither against Christ nor for Him.

SECTION IV

PREPARATION FOR OPENING THE SCROLL

Chapters 4 and 5

1 An observation about the understanding of events

The histories that have been written about countries, peoples, and movements are concerned with events that have taken place in the past. Their origin, their meaning, and their future are usually seen in purely human, historical, and earthly terms. Seldom does the historian try to relate human history to divine concern and superintendence. The line of his vision is entirely horizontal.

The Revelation of John is also concerned with events, though future rather than past events. Its visions were given 'to show his servants what must soon take place' (1:1). In the first vision John was instructed to write down what is and what is to take place hereafter' (1:19). In the next vision he heard the same voice telling him, 'Come up and I will show you what must take place after this' (4:1). These events had, in fact, already begun to take place. They concerned the suffering and victory of the people of God as a result of their conflict with the powers of this age. They were 'the tribulation and the kingdom and the patient endurance' which through his exile on Patmos John was already sharing with other Christians (1:9).

There is a major difference, however, between the manner in which John describes events that are to take place and the manner in which historians describe events that have taken place. The events which the historians describe did indeed 'take place', but their understanding of these events is limited to people, forces, and circumstances on earth that caused them. The experience of the Church which John sees, on the other hand, takes place 'in Jesus'. He is concerned with events that are inseparably connected with the history of the kingdom of heaven.

Therefore the events which he relates have not only a horizontal but also, and especially, a vertical meaning. The struggle of the Church takes place 'in Jesus', and Jesus has a place in the struggle. That is why the history of the City of God is written differently from the history of the city of man. Psalm 46:5-7 speaks eloquently of this divine aspect. Therefore the vision that begins the description of the events 'that must soon take place' is not a vision of persecution, suffering, and death. It is one of heavenly majesty, great peace, inexpressible power, divine authority, boundless joy, and total control of all that is to be. The vision set forth in Revelation 4 and 5 represents the blessed reality in heaven that lies behind, governs, and uses for good the often tragic realities on earth. With this knowledge and therefore with this comfort, the Church moves into the future and on to the End. Before the battle is fought, the victory has been achieved. For this reason Jesus encourages His followers again and again with the certainty of their victory: 'Fear not, little flock, for it is the Father's good pleasure to give you the kingdom' (Luke 12:32), or again, 'In this world you have tribulation, but be of good cheer, I have overcome the world' (John 16:33).

2 The throne of power, chapter 4

When the vision recorded in chapter 1 had been revealed, John was next shown an open door in heaven. The idea of heaven opened was not new to the Jewish prophet (Ezekiel 1:1, Mark 1:10, John 1:51). A voice called him to come up to heaven like that which called Moses to come to God on the top of Mount Sinai (Exodus 19:20). As this heavenly vision unfolded before him, John saw a throne standing and 'one seated on the throne'. A throne is the ceremonial seat of a king, the symbol of authority, power, majesty, and judgment that pertains to his high office. The Occupant of the throne is not described. The pious Jew would not pronounce the name of God; much less could John describe the Kingly Majesty which his eyes saw. He could only compare God to the beauty of precious stones: the dark-red crimson of carnelian, the polished white of jasper. The whole of the divine presence seemed to John to consist of such costly, dazzling brilliance.

The further description of the throne-scene consists of the rainbow, the twenty-four elders, emanations from the throne, the seven torches, the sea of glass before the throne, and the four living creatures that surround it. In the biblical view, the rainbow is more than an appearance in the sky of great beauty and majesty. It is also a symbol of God's faithfulness in holding to His promise not again to destroy the earth with a flood (Genesis 9:8-17). It is a symbol of God's covenant faithfulness. The elders are not identified beyond the statement that each has a throne, that they are dressed in white robes, have crowns on their heads, and are twenty-four in number. These descriptions are, however, significant. The thrones indicate rulership, the crowns victory and authority, the white robes purity. Among the symbolical numbers used in Scripture twenty-four is a multiple of twelve, which is a frequently used number for symbolical purposes in the Bible. In Revelation alone the number twelve appears more than twenty times. Of these, four are very suggestive in the present connection. The new Jerusalem, which is described in chapter 21, has twelve gates and on the gates the names of the twelve tribes of the sons of Israel are engraved. The wall of the city has twelve foundations and on them the twelve names of the apostles of the Lamb are inscribed (verses 12-14). It is therefore probable that the twenty-four elders represent the heavenly assembly of the Old Testament saints of Israel and the New Testament saints of the Church. In their heavenly state they are 'more than conquerors' through Him who loved them (Romans 8:37).

From the throne of God, lightnings, voices, and peals of thunder proceed. They suggest the formidable power of the authority which the throne represents. Before it seven torches burn to represent the seven spirits of God which point to the fulness of light in the Holy Spirit. Common though glass is among us today, in New Testament times it was an exceptional commodity and was regarded as precious. That the entire floor of a throne-room should be made of glass was hardly conceivable. Its extension before the throne of God impressed John as a crystal sea on which stood the throne of the Almighty Ruler of the universe.

The four living creatures take their character from the

first chapters of Ezekiel and from the sixth chapter of Isaiah. They are, however, greatly simplified, as a reading of the passages in Ezekiel and Isaiah will show. Learned studies have been made of the possible origin of these figures, tracing them back as far as Babylonian astronomy. John's purpose, however, was to impart meanings rather than origins. They represented a type of angel known as cherub, better known to us in the plural as cherubim (Ezekiel 10:1ff), and seraph, also better known in the plural as seraphim (Isaiah 6:1ff). They were winged, probably possessed animal bodies and sometimes human, sometimes animal heads. Special high functions were given to them by God as the executors of His will. The key to understanding their function in Revelation is found in an ancient rabbinical statement, 'There are four holding the chief place in the world—among creatures, man; among birds, the eagle; among cattle, the ox; among beasts, the lion.' The lion is the majestic head of the wild animal kingdom; the ox the representative of the domestic animal kingdom; man is the representative of the intelligent creation; and the eagle the lordly master of the winged animal world and the king of the skies. The four represented, in the form of cherubim and seraphim, the entirety of God's living creation. Their eyes see both far around and deeply into God's vast creation. They are, however, as suggested in Isaiah 6, clothed with two wings of reverence (they do not behold God directly), two wings of humility (they are not worthy to be seen by God), and two wings of service (they go where God commands them to go). As such they form a sharp contrast to the beasts or living creatures which we find in Revelation 13, and in Daniel 7. There the brutal demonic character of the creatures indicates how the goodness and nobility of the heavenly being can be transformed into blasphemy and tyranny.

These mighty angels surrounding the throne never cease to sing the praises of God, who made them and all things. As they do so, the elders join them and bring the worship of redeemed men to honour the Creator. They cast their crowns before God to testify that it was not they but He who gave them the victory over sin and death and the powers of hell. The praise that men and angels render to God is not merely in the form of song or music. It is rather the testimony of the whole of creation and redemption to the beauty, the power, and the wisdom of God. It must be remembered that the four creatures and the twenty-four elders are symbols. There are no angels with varied heads, six wings, and eyes behind and in front of them before the throne of God. Nor are there twenty-four elders in white robes there seated on thrones. Indeed, there is no throne with thunders and lightnings and voices in heaven. This is all symbolic language which we must try to understand in terms of God's two great works: creation and redemption. The four creatures represent God's creative work; the twenty-four elders His redemptive work in the Old and in the New Dispensation. What their common praise means is expressed eloquently in the last verse of Psalm 103, 'Bless the Lord, all his works, in all places of his dominion. Bless the Lord, O my soul!'

3 The scroll with seven seals, chapter 5

Having observed the majestic and overwhelming scene in the heavenly palace, John's vision returns to Him who sits on the throne. In His right hand, that is, in God's right hand of power, John sees a scroll. It is so full of writing that it overflows, as it were, to the reverse side. What is written in it cannot be read, however, for the scroll is sealed with seven seals.

The scroll was the book-form of the ancient world. The name is derived from the early English word 'scrowle' or 'rowle', meaning roll. It consisted of strips of papyrus or leather from twelve to eighteen inches wide pasted together to form a length of about thirty feet. This was fastened at each end to round wooden pins on which it could be rolled and unrolled. Even today this idea of the roll-form persists in the English word 'volume', derived from the Latin *volumen*, meaning a roll of writing.

Such was the form of the mysterious book that John saw in the hand of God. Surely such a writing, completely sealed with seven seals of divine authority, must contain matters of great importance. Only one who is qualified by understanding and worth can open such a book and disclose its contents. Therefore a strong angel came forward asking with a loud voice, 'Who is worthy to open the roll and break its seals?' No one responded to this call of the mighty angel. In all of heaven and all of earth none was found worthy of receiving and unsealing the book. On seeing no one come forward to open the scroll and break its seal, John wept for sorrow.

When we understand what is meant by 'opening' the scroll and 'breaking' its seals, we shall sympathize with John's sorrow. What is at issue here is not a simple breaking of seals and reading a piece of writing. That any court clerk can do. Rather the question is, 'Who is able to understand and to interpret what is written in the book?' John doubtless sensed that this book had much to do with the fulfillment of the promise given in Revelation 1 to disclose the things that would soon take place. But now there was no one to reveal the contents of it or to interpret their meaning. Then one of the twenty-four elders came forward and comforted him: the Lion of the tribe of Judah, the Root of David, has conquered so that he is worthy to open the scroll, break its seven seals, and reveal its content.

On hearing this, John sees what he had not seen before. In the midst of the throne, the elders, and the four living creatures, he sees standing the figure of a lamb. Known for its harmlessness and gentleness, the lamb is a perfect picture of unresisting submission to sacrifice. Therefore Jesus is compared to a lamb, notably in the familiar figure found in Isaiah 53, 'like a lamb that is led to the slaughter and like a sheep that before its shearers is dumb, so he opened not his mouth.' This Lamb, however, while fully lamblike, gentle, and unresisting, is at the same time mighty and victorious. His power lies in complete and uncompromising obedience to the will of the Father. For this He is rewarded by being given a name that is above every name, before whom every knee shall bow in heaven and on earth (Philippians 2:11). For this reason the Lamb is an unusual lamb. He has seven horns and seven eyes. When the word 'horn' is used in a figurative or symbolical sense in the Bible, it often means strength, might. The horn of the feared bush cow is its chief weapon. Especially in the visions of Daniel and Revelation is the word so used. The weak Lamb, therefore, has perfect strength in the seven horns set in His head. Moreover, His power is supported by His knowledge of all that happens in the world, as represented by His seven all-seeing eyes. These qualities make Jesus the omnipotent and omniscient

World Ruler. The sacrificial Lamb is also a Conqueror who is justly named the Lion of the tribe of Judah, the descendant of David the king of Israel, who was a type of the mighty son to be born in his line.

When the conquering Lamb takes the scroll out of the hand of Him who sits on the throne, the four great creatures that surround the throne and the twenty-four elders fall down before the Lamb and worship. They sing 'a new song' declaring Him worthy to open the scroll because He has been sacrificed and by his death has redeemed men for God from every tribe, people, tongue, and nation. These He has formed into a kingdom and a priesthood that shall reign on the earth.

Suddenly the power of the scene and the song is re-enforced a thousand times as myriads upon myriads of angels join the four creatures and the elders, singing a seven-fold doxology to the Lamb. Thereupon these are joined by every other creature in heaven and on earth and under the earth as they ascribe to the Father and to the Lamb blessing and honour and glory and might for ever and ever. These mighty choruses the four angels and the elders conclude as they kneel and speak the final Amen, meaning Truly, Surely, It is so.

Meaning for today
The things that are about to be revealed to John are in every way terrible for the world; they are terrible for the Church. They are, in a sense, even more terrible for the Church than for the world. The Church must endure a double portion of suffering. Because it is a part of the world and of the society in which its members live, the people of God will suffer along with all others in the judgments which God will inflict on the natural and social orders as a result of men's unbelief. These judgments are described by the seals of the scroll in God's right hand, by the seven trumpet blasts which follow the seven seals, and by the seven last plagues which follow the seven trumpets. Many of these judgments will affect the Church as well as the world. All this in addition to the severe persecution which it will suffer for Christ's sake.

This whole series of natural disasters for the world and bitter persecution for the Church is preceded by the majestic throne-room scene which John has described.

The Church faces its suffering in the world with this knowledge of the throne and its divine Occupant, who rules over all. When persecution overtakes it, the Church knows that even the persecution that kills is not the final word in its life. The final word is with Him who is seated on the throne and with the Lord Jesus Christ, who shares the throne of power with Him. In front of that throne is a sea of calm and peace. Around that throne the whole creation unites in the praise of Him who made all things. There the Church praises its Redeemer and Lord. There Church and creation and angels ascribe blessing and honour and glory and might to Him who sits on the throne and to the Lamb for ever and ever.

But there is more, much more, that the Church knows as it passes through its trials. Though it is weak and has no strength of its own, there is a vast heavenly power which, unseen, protects it and surrounds it. It is the power revealed in the scroll sealed with seven seals. It is the power that comes out of the seals in the form of the seven trumpets. It is the power that comes out of the seven trumpets in the form of the seven last plagues. The scroll in heaven controls what happens on earth. The scroll in heaven interprets what happens on earth. The scroll in heaven sets limits to the power and the hostility of the world. The scroll in heaven sets limits to the suffering of the Church.

The purpose of the vision of the throne-room and the scroll is to prepare God's people for suffering, defeat, and death. It does so by showing them the heavenly power, the victory, and the wisdom that watches over their trials on earth. The Lamb who died for them is now their King and their Protector. The secret of both the Church's patience and victory is its knowledge of that other world where its life 'is hidden with Christ in God'. This is the world about which the historians and the newspapers and the news magazines do not write. This is the world about which the politicians and the scientists and the businessmen do not speak. They are all very much concerned about secret documents and secret treaties; they are not concerned about the secret scroll of God in which the real meaning of so much of history and science and commerce and state-craft is found. The world is very much interested in reports about the meetings of heads of state, and conferences of international financiers, military strategists, and economists. It is little interested in the plan of God for the world and in the execution of it by the Lord Jesus Christ. But this truly great and profitable knowledge was revealed to John, and through him to all who follow in the path of the suffering, death and victory of the Lamb. This knowledge is peace, as Jesus said:

> Peace I leave with you; my peace I give to you; not as the world gives do I give to you. Let not your hearts be troubled, neither let them be afraid. You heard me say to you, 'I go away, and I will come to you.' If you loved me you would have rejoiced, because I go to the Father; for the Father is greater than I. And now I have told you before it takes place, so that when it does take place, you may believe.

(John 14:27-29)

The vision of the throne-room and the scroll has been revealed to us so that as the scroll is being fulfilled we may believe in the Power that watches over its execution.

THE OPENING OF THE SCROLL

Chapter 6

The opening of the scroll begins the description of three groups of judgments. These are the contents of the seven seals, of the seven trumpets, and of the seven last plagues. The seven trumpets arise out of the seventh seal, and the seven last plagues arise out of the seventh trumpet. Thus there is a continuous line connecting twenty-one judgments, from the first judgment of the seals to the last judgment of the plagues.

1 The scroll and the problem of evil

The sealed scroll speaks of things that are about to happen. This may lead some to think that the scroll represents God's eternal decree of which both Christian and Islamic theology speak. This decree is generally referred to as God's predestination of all things that are to happen. Such a reading of the scroll, however, would be a complete misunderstanding of its meaning. The seals of chapter 6, the trumpets of chapters 8 and 9, and the seven last plagues described in chapters 15 and 16 speak only of judgments of God.

There is more to history than the judgments of God on the evil of the world. There are also the peaceful years from birth to death which millions are privileged to live, the growth of the Church in numbers and in understanding, the history of nations, the achievements of culture, the development of the world's resources, the advance of learning and skills and exploration of the universe. Revelation itself speaks clearly of them: the kings of the earth shall bring the glory and honour of the nations into the new Jerusalem (Revelation 21:22-27). The kings who bring this glory into the new Jerusalem are the kings not only of political empires, but also of the empires of music, art, literature, science, commerce, and thought. The books and the instruments and the sculptures and the buildings in which these achievements find expression in the history of mankind shall all perish But their making and their use have enriched the spirit of mankind, and this spiritual deposit shall through the Church enter the new creation. If the scroll represented God's decree, then such matters and many more would also have to be mentioned.

The scroll, therefore, is simply a preview of what is to happen with respect to God's judgments on the world and the suffering of the Church in the world. But this preview is not merely for information. It has been given for comfort, for hope, for encouragement, and as a call to repentance. The world will describe the things that are about to happen as events, disasters, catastrophes, calamities. The Church, on the other hand, will see them as acts of God, divine judgments, heavenly protection for believers, chastisements for those who love God, preludes to joy and peace, the forerunners of final victory over all things evil. Therefore Jesus said, 'There will be signs in the sun and moon and stars, and upon the earth distress of nations . . . men fainting with fear and with foreboding of what is coming on the world. . . . Now when these things begin to take place, look up and raise your heads, because your redemption is drawing near' (Luke 21:25-28).

The Christian community must clearly understand that God does not decree sword and famine and conquest and war and pestilence and death and Hades. He did not create them; He did not plan them; He did not ordain them. All are opposed to him; all deny the goodness and the righteousness and the holiness for which God stands. The existence of evil is a mystery that Scripture nowhere explains. The excellence of the cosmic Christ is not that He brought an explanation of evil, but that He conquered it. He met sin and evil and death and hell and defeated them. The glory of the gospel is not an explanation of sin, but the declaration of its total conquest by the incarnate, crucified, and risen Lord.

The purpose of Revelation is a limited one. It wants to show the power and the love and the justice of God that lie behind the afflictions which the Church must often endure in this world. God opens the heavens and reveals its glories to us to comfort and sustain His saints in their hour of trial.

2 The breaking of the seals

Each of the first four seals produces a rider on a horse. They are known as the four horsemen of the Apocalypse. The Old Testament background of the four horses is doubtless Zechariah 1:7-11. In Revelation the riders are more fully described than in Zechariah. As the horsemen in Zechariah go out 'to patrol the earth', so the horsemen in Revelation go out to afflict the earth.

a. The rider on the white horse, verses 1,2

Only the first horse and its rider are pleasant to see. Neither blood nor death, neither suffering nor famine characterize them. There is only the white horse (a sign of victory) and the rider with a bow (a military weapon) in his hand and a crown (sign of victory and authority) on his head. He goes out conquering and to conquer. The battles that secure the conquests are not described. The significant expression in the passage is 'he went out'. The picture intended is that of an army leaving the homeland to attack and conquer an enemy. Ranks are unbroken, uniforms cleaned and pressed, weapons shining, equipment in prime order. Isaiah describes such a newly trained and newly equipped army:

> None is weary, none stumbles,
> none slumbers or sleeps,
> not a wastecloth is loose,
> not a sandal-thong broken.
> Their arrows are sharp, all their bows bent,
> their horses' hoofs seem like flint,
> and their wheels like the whirlwind. (5:27,28)

This is the bright, the attractive side of military life, the aspect that makes boys want to be soldiers. The army that marches out to conquer does not show the dark side of its beauty:

> Their roaring is like a lion,
> like young lions they roar,
> they growl and seize their prey,
> they carry it off and none can rescue. (5:29,30)

It does not reveal 'the boot of the tramping warrior in

battle tumult and every garment rolled in blood'
(Isaiah 9:5).

It is tempting to identify the rider on the white horse
with Christ, who also rides a white horse in victory
(19:11-16). In fact, a number of writers on Revelation
believe the figure should be so understood. There is
nothing in Revelation 6, however, to warrant this identification. The rider on the white horse is one of four horsemen who have throughout human history afflicted the
earth The pain and suffering which follow behind the
rider on the white horse become clear when the second
seal is broken.

b. The rider on the red horse, verses 3,4
This horseman represents the previous horseman in
action. He is the horseman of war who is permitted to take
peace from the earth, to set nation against nation, so that
men kill each other. This they do with the 'sword', the
age-old symbol of every kind of military weapon. That this
action is 'permitted' indicates the hidden power whereby
Christ controls the extent to which the war-lords of the
earth can assert their power. The terrible cost of war in
lives and materials lost or damaged is beyond description.
In World War 1, 1914-1918, 65,000,000 men in all were
mobilized in the armies and navies of the warring powers.
Of these, 8,500,000, or more than 12%, were killed.
21,000,000, or 33%, were wounded. Nearly 8,000,000, or
11%, were taken prisoners. These make a total of
37,500,000, or 57%, casualties. This does not include
civilians killed and wounded or civilians sick and
dead due to famine and other causes related to war.
Nor do these figures measure the suffering and the
humiliation of the conquered, the abuse of victory, the
fearful financial cost, and the unmeasurable extent of
destroyed and damaged property.

c. The rider on the black horse, verses 5,6
Sometimes as a result of war, but usually quite apart
from it, famine comes to deny to men the food which they
need to live. The black horse represents this affliction.
He carries a rider who holds a balance in his hand. This
balance or weighing-scales would appear to be a symbol of
food scarcity. Usually grain is sold by measure; now it will

be carefully weighed. A voice comes from among the four angels who represent creation, or the natural order that produces food and drink. It warns of a scarcity of food which is best described by the translation of the New English Bible:

A whole day's wage for a quart of flour,
a whole day's wage for three quarts of barley.

With this a man will have to feed himself and his family. But where shall he obtain money for clothes, shoes, and other necessities of life?

The judgment of the black horse, like that of the pale horse, is not final or complete. Oil and wine remain in supply. Similarly the rider on the pale horse has power over only one fourth of the earth. The judgments are meant to lead men to repentance and are therefore restrained and partial.

d. The rider on the pale horse, verses 7,8

The last of the horses to be called out is pale in colour. What the word 'pale' intends to convey here is the colour of death, which will vary according to racial skin colour. The word 'pale' best suited the Palestinian idea of the death colour. The rider who sits on the horse is Death and he is followed by another named Hades. In the New Testament, Hades (like Sheol in the Old Testament) is the place of the dead. These figures of Death and Hades represent unnatural death resulting from unnatural causes. Those mentioned are death by violence, by famine, by rapidly spreading disease, and by wild beasts. These were examples suited to the time of John. The two riders, Death and Hades, were given power over a fourth part of the earth. When one considers all the causes of death apart from sickness and old age, the figure of 'one-fourth' may not be far wrong. As a symbolic figure, however, it suggests a large part, a substantial portion, rather than a mathematical fraction.

e. The souls under the altar, verses 9-11

When the four horsemen pass off the scene, the fifth seal is opened. It reveals to John a strange and moving sight. He sees the 'souls', in a number not indicated, who have been killed because of persecution for Christ's sake. As he sees them, he hears them crying out to God to delay no longer the avenging of their blood on those who have killed them. The time for the exercise of the divine justice, however, has not yet come, and they are asked to be patient.

No doubt the strangest feature of this vision is the position of the souls 'under the altar'. The strangeness only indicates our distance from the Jewish thought and worship with which John was so familiar. For the Jew the life or the soul of a person was in the blood. The classic text is Leviticus 17:11, 'For the life of the flesh is in the blood.' The Hebrew word for life in this passage is *nephesh*, which is also the word used for soul. Life, blood, and soul are inseparably related in Hebrew thought. In sacrificing the daily burnt-offering, the priest had to perform several actions with the blood of the sacrificial animal. When he had done so, 'the rest of the blood he shall pour out at the base of the altar of burnt-offering which is at the door of the tent of meeting' (Leviticus 4:7). This was to show that the life was given to God, for the smoke from the altar on which the animal was sacrificed ascended to God. The base of the altar was therefore always red with the blood (i.e. with the souls) of the victims that had been thrown against it.

The souls represented as sacrificed for the sake of Christ cry out to God for vengeance on their persecutors. Such a thought is expressed in Scripture for the first time in Genesis 4:10, which speaks of the blood of murdered Abel as crying to God from the ground against his brother Cain. The legitimacy of such a cry will be discussed later in Part 3.

The request of the martyred souls was not denied, but they were asked to wait. Persecution must first run its course. Then all who have suffered on Christ's account will be vindicated together. The final judgment of God on sin is one, not piecemeal. So, in the end, is salvation. Those who have preceded us will not be made perfect without those who come after them (Hebrews 11:39,40).

f. The end of the age, verses 12-17
The sixth seal represents the very last days of man's existence on the earth. There are catastrophic events in nature, and there is total dismay among men. The earth quakes, the sun, moon, stars, and sky are profoundly

affected. Mountains are removed, islands vanish. In all apocalyptic descriptions nature takes a terrifying part in the events of the End-time.

Men see these things and tremble. So great is the universal fear that no one is excepted. Kings and emperors, the great men of business, the wealthy, heads of armies, slave and freeman—all seek cover from the approaching calamity. Their fear is not of death or physical harm. Indeed, they seek death. They want the mountains to fall on them and the rocks to cover them. They have seen God seated on the throne, they have seen the wrath of the Lamb, and they are unable to stand before them. They want to hide from the face of God and of the Lamb, and they consider death to be the only hiding place. The same revelation that gave comfort, hope, and encouragement to the Church brings terror and despair to those who do not know Christ. This response of the world to the manifestation of God's wrath is a characteristic feature of apocalyptic writing.

The seventh seal is broken in chapter 8. It does not contain an independent judgment of its own as the first six have. Instead it introduces a new series of judgments in the form of seven trumpet blasts which set loose afflictions on earth. Chapter 7 shows how God's people are protected from these judgments.

Meaning for today

There are few chapters in Revelation which speak more to our time than chapter 6. In books, in newspapers, in magazine accounts, in radio broadcasts we read and hear about the four horsemen who are riding across the earth today. We hear the cry for justice. We sense that some time there must be a judgment in which guilty men will not be able to escape. These are things all men understand.

In the second half of the twentieth century the rider on the white horse is the fearful military complex that prepares for nuclear war. The shining missiles with warheads ready, the complicated firing pads, the aeroplanes that deliver bombs, and the smartly uniformed officers and men are all admirable representatives of technology and military fitness—but they are deadly. The sword of smaller wars has been given into the hands of now this nation, group, or tribe, now that. Many fight for justice and are killed in the struggle. Their blood cries out for judgment from battle fields, from forest paths, from rice paddies, and from ruined cities. Car, train, and aeroplane accidents, theft, murder, disease, pollution of the air, rivers seas, and soil are the common experience of all modern nations. Famine may stalk a whole continent from east to west. And in it all, there is the hope of the just and the fear of the guilty.

Nevertheless, to say these things is not the message of the sixth chapter of Revelation. These experiences come to every generation in forms suited to their day. We have all in our own way and in our own time seen the rider on the white horse on parade, the death and destruction caused by the rider on the red horse, and all the rest. So far as reporting or describing these things is concerned, Revelation does not tell us anything new. In short, *these* things do not have to be revealed. We know them. In fact, they were there before John wrote about them.

What then is new here? What is being revealed in chapter 6 that we cannot know without revelation from God? Why is this chapter a proper and highly significant part of the book that is called Revelation? The thing that is new here is the meaning of the events that the opened seals report. The new, the wonderfully new, matter that is reported here is that the *Lamb* breaks the seals that introduce these dark events. All the events that flow out of the broken seals are in His hand. He permits them. He controls them. He limits them. And He stops them when they have served their purpose. That is what the books and the newspapers and the magazines and the radio broadcasts do not tell us. They can see and report the work of the four horsemen and the injustices which they commit and the call for punishment which this creates. They do not see or understand or believe that the slain Lamb of God is the King of the universe. This is the hidden wisdom that the powers that rule the world have never known. The wisdom for which the world has an eye is the insight of the statesman, the discovery of the scientist, the strategy of the general. The wisdom that governs the believer is a gift of the Holy Spirit which enables him to see the eternal realities of heaven behind the passing realities of earth. Central in the purpose of

Christ is the completion of His Church. He will create a new heaven and a new earth in which righteousness will dwell. This is the knowledge that comforts the people of God and puts limits to our trust in the wisdom and the opinions of even good men. It limits our fear of the cruelty and injustice of the wicked, but creates trust without limit in Him who is the Ruler of all.

With this the question arises: how can the good God make use of evil forces and evil men? How can the terrible forces represented by the four horsemen be used to serve God's kingdom? How must we understand that Christ allows His mighty angels to say 'Come' to the powers that bring sorrow and destruction? This will be discussed in Section VIII, Parts 3, 4, 5, and 6, in connection with the judgments of the seven trumpets.

Truth is a circle from which mankind, even in its greatest rebellion against God, is unable to escape. Within that circle man can resist, oppose, and deny the truth, but he can never escape from the circle. He cannot destroy the truth. He cannot break its power. Always he will at the end of his struggle collide with and be broken by the iron ring that surrounds his life. He may die victorious in evil; his death simply introduces him to a higher court of judgment. In the end, as Jesus said, we can do nothing against the truth, but only for the truth. God makes even the wrath of men to praise Him. He catches the wise in their wisdom. This is the riches and the wisdom and the knowledge of God. This is the mystery of the power and the judgments of God, which surround His people in this life and bring them at last to rest in the life that is to come.

It is in this light that we must understand the souls under the altar crying out to God for judgment on their unrepentant persecutors. Justice will prevail, for it is an essential aspect of the truth. Crime unpunished leaves the impression of the victory of darkness over light. We who are limited in our vision and cannot see the end from the beginning do not have the patience that God has. Therefore, we seek to protect the threatened truth, and set limits to the advancing chaos. But God sees the whole of the battle. He sees the relationships of all the sectors of the battlefront to each other. For this reason He is able to wait for the strategic moment to make the final and decisive attack on the powers of evil.

The souls under the altar are not therefore loveless and vindictive people who are unwilling to forgive and forget. They are simply, as all believers are, citizens of a kingdom in which it is proper and necessary for wrong to be judged and the rule of law to be upheld. Those who scorn the love of the Lamb will have to face the wrath of the Lamb. It is this wrath which in the end protects the circle of truth that surrounds the universe and all that is in it.

PREPARATION FOR BLOWING THE SEVEN TRUMPETS

Chapter 7

The writer of Revelation is a master artist who creatively follows the principles of good writing. He does not try to say everything at once. He is like a builder who progresses purposefully from foundation to walls to roof, and then turns to the internal structure of floors, ceilings, doors, and windows. When both external and internal structure stand, he applies the over-all decorations and the house is complete. The house is *envisioned* in its entirety before the construction, it is *lived in* in its entirety after construction, but the actual construction takes place piece by piece. John, having received the disclosure of God's purpose as a whole, put it together section by section and at last gave to the Church this wonderful book in its entirety.

Chapter 7 is a good illustration of the gradual and progressive way in which he planned and wrote the book. The chapter speaks about the protection which God's people receive when God afflicts the world with His judgments. This means that in the suffering that the world will endure as a result of the trumpet blasts (chapters 8 and 9), the Church will be kept from making sinful responses to them. But it also means that God's people will be protected in the same way against the suffering inflicted by the four horsemen that have already appeared. Similarly, we must remember that the four horsemen are *always* riding through the earth, and the cry for justice in persecution is *always* being made by the persecuted. This would also appear to be the meaning of the trumpet blasts (chapters 8 and 9) and the seven last plagues (chapters 15 and 16). These do not simply follow the breaking of the seals. They are a part of the scroll with seven seals. The seven trumpets come out of the seventh seal, and the seven plagues come out of the seventh trumpet. All three groups of judgments are happening at the same time. John, however, must necessarily describe them, as also the background in heaven that controls them, one by one, that is to say, one after the other. In our reading of Revelation, therefore, we should be aware of the unity of time in which all are taking place. With a few exceptions like 6:12-17, the seals, the trumpets, the plagues, and the protection of believers against their judgments are contemporaneous.

The three groups of judgment also represent the judging and restraining action of God on sin from quite different points of view. The seals reveal wholly external physical judgments. The trumpets reveal both external physical and internal spiritual judgments. The seven bowls of the wrath of God are also both external and internal in their effect. Further, there is progress in the severity of the judgments. In the judgments of the seals Death and Hades received power over one fourth of the earth. In the judgments of the trumpets the area of judgment is increased to one third of land and sea and sky and mankind. In the judgments of the seven bowls no limits are placed anywhere, and when the last bowl is poured out, a great voice cries, 'It is done!'

1 The five angels, verses 1-3

The judgments of God that are to afflict mankind are represented as winds coming from the four corners of the earth. The 'winds' in question are presumably storms, cyclones, hurricanes—the kind of winds that can inflict severe damage. As we shall see in chapter 8, the winds represent judgments of various kinds. They may or may not include the natural occurrence of powerful winds. These judgments are represented as being controlled by angels. Again, the description is symbolical. In the Bible as a whole, the judgments of God are sent by God himself. Here, however, the emphasis is on the fact that the judgments are controlled. When, where, and how judgments come, lies in the hands of God. This hand or power of God is here represented in the form of angels. They stand at the four 'corners' or directions from which the winds come, namely east, west, north, south. These angels are holding back the winds that would be hurtful to the earth or the sea or to trees. Special mention is made of trees both because they are often uprooted by storms and because they are a symbol of nature's usefulness. Trees provide wood, fire, shade, fruit, beauty, and as forests they are an important factor in controlling climate and rainfall.

A fifth angel now ascends from the east who has in his hand the seal of the living God. He represents the protective power of God. Similarly, two other angels with specific functions are mentioned in Revelation. One is the angel of fire (14:18), and the other the angel of water (16:5). Whether winds or protection or fire or water—all are in God's power and this power is represented in the form of angels who exercise it. The angel arising in the east instructs the angels who control the winds to restrain them. He must first seal the servants of God on their foreheads. Those who are sealed cannot be hurt by the destroying angel. One is reminded of the angel of death passing over the houses of the Israelites that were marked with the blood of a lamb and entering the houses of the Egyptians to slay the firstborn (Exodus 12:21-30). The seal is figuratively placed on the foreheads of believers in the same way that slaves in the ancient world were often branded by their masters to show to whom they belonged. The servants of God who are sealed are in fact slaves of God and they bear His mark of ownership.

The seal that was put on the foreheads of God's people was the name of God (7:3;22:4), or the name of God and of the Lamb (14:1). By 'name' is meant more than a designation such as our names are. In Scripture the name of God is God Himself, God in His revelation, God in His power. 'The name of the Lord is a strong tower; the righteous man flees into it and is safe' (Proverbs 18:10). For this reason the protection that God gives is not in the first place physical protection against earthquake or pestilence or imprisonment or death. Nor is the seal placed on the physical foreheads of believers. It is spiritual in character. The 'sealing' of the servants of God means that the judgments of God on the world, however severe, will not be allowed to destroy or harm the believers' relationship to God. Therefore Paul says that nothing in all creation will be able to separate us from the love of God in Christ Jesus our Lord (Romans 8:38,39). It was also with this in mind that Jesus said about the tribulation of the End-time that those days would be shortened for the sake of the elect, lest they also should be led astray (Matthew 24:21-24; Mark 13:19-23). No one can snatch them out of His hand, for the Father who has given them to Him is greater than all, and no one is able to snatch them out of the Father's hand (John 10:28,29).

2 The sealing of the one hundred and forty-four thousand, verses 4-8

John makes Israel a picture of the Church in her fulness. Twelve thousand are sealed from each of the twelve tribes. As the number seven results from the addition of three and four, so the number twelve results from their multiplication. Three and four were highly sacred numbers in the ancient Semitic world. Both play an important role in the natural order. Family (father, mother, child), tree (roots, trunk, branches), water (liquid, steam, ice), and any natural process (beginning, middle, end) may be mentioned as examples of the appearance of threes. The significance of four is seen especially in the four directions of the compass. It signifies the totality of creation. When three and four are multiplied to form twelve, the idea of fulness is emphasised. This is further re-enforced by the number thousand, which is the three-fold multiple of ten. This number, too, is used symbolically in the sense of a rounded whole, such as the ten commandments and a tenth of a harvest or of one's income (the tithe). Three times four times twelve times one thousand makes, therefore, for a fulness of great symbolical significance, namely the one hundred and forty-four thousand who are sealed, representing the family of God of all times and places.[1]

---

[1] In the theology of Jehovah's Witnesses the saved are divided into two groups, the 'anointed ones' or the 144,000 (Revelation 7:4-8), and the 'other sheep'. The 144,000 are the spiritual elite and they will dwell with Christ for ever in heaven. The 'other sheep' are saved but they have not made the sacrifices that the 144,000 have. They are, one might say, second-class believers. They will never have spiritual bodies but will live in Paradise on earth after Armageddon. The worldwide Church as it has existed since the time of the apostles is hopelessly corrupt; it is the harlot of Revelation 17. Only the 144,000 and the 'other sheep' will live in the next life. All others will be exterminated.

There is some irregularity in the names given to the twelve tribes. There are fourteen lists of the tribes in the Bible, thirteen of them in the Old Testament. No list agrees with any other in the order of the names, and there are differences also in the names themselves. Some list Levi, Joseph, and Ephraim, while others do not mention them. In the list in Revelation Judah is mentioned first instead of Reuben, doubtless because of Jesus' descent from David of the tribe of Judah. Levi, who is usually omitted, is named and Joseph takes the place of his son Ephraim. Dan is not mentioned, some say because it was believed that the Anti-Christ was to come from the tribe of Dan. These differences, however, are irrelevant to the purposes of the writer. That purpose was to present a perfect number of the saved in a way that any reader familiar with the Old Testament would be able to understand.

✱

3 The great multitude, verses 9-17
At this point John leaves the imagery of the Old Testament. He now sees a great throng of every tribe and race and language standing before the throne praising God and the Lamb. This is the New Testament description of the fulness of the Church to which the one hundred and forty-four thousand, who are sealed from Israel's tribes, point. They are clothed in the white robes of salvation and have palm branches in their hands. They represent the totality of the redeemed, all the 'servants of God' of all time. In verse 14 they are described in a more limited way as 'they who have come out of the great tribulation'. Does this mean that there is another company of the redeemed in heaven who have not been in any tribulation? Or is the life of any Christian on earth a form of tribulation? In 14:1-5 the one hundred and forty-four thousand are again referred to but no mention is made of their suffering in persecution. They are chaste, they follow the Lamb wherever He goes, they have been redeemed from mankind as first-fruits for God and the Lamb, and in their mouths no lie was found. In verses 15-17, in which one of the heavenly elders describes the great multitude before the throne, no specific reference is made to persecution. They shall hunger and thirst no more; the sun shall not smite them with scorching heat; and God will wipe

away all tears from their eyes. This is a description of the removal of the earthly pain which any serious Christian leaves behind when he joins the Church triumphant. Usually, however, when John speaks of Christian suffering he has persecution in mind.

Meaning for today

There is a word which describes the deepest concern that many people have today. It is *security*. They want the assurance that they will keep the good things and conditions which they have and if possible increase them. They want security for their jobs and careers, security for their place in the community, security for their health, security for old age, security for their children, security for the national well-being and defence. Many means are used to achieve this security: education with its certificates and qualifications, hard work, economic planning, insurance, pensions, health planning, improved and ever higher education, budgets for national defence, and so much more. When something occurs which threatens the safeguards that have been erected, every effort is made and all forces are mobilized to restore the endangered security.

In all the concern for security that surrounds us, there is a form of security that one hears little about. It is the security of our relationship to God. Yet it is the greatest of all securities, for it alone is a security that will continue, and what it guards is the best and deepest thing in life. Jesus said, 'What will it profit a man if he gains the whole world but loses his own soul?' Again and again the Bible warns us to seek the things of primary worth and make them our greatest interest. Therefore we must first seek the kingdom of God and its righteousness, and all these other things will find their proper place.

This security is moral, spiritual security. It is a security of a religious nature. More specifically, it is security of a Christian religious nature. Because of this, it is not a security that we can do anything to guarantee. No educational certification, no amount of money in the bank, no insurance policy, no personal, community, or national planning, no power of national defence, not even the Church with all its spiritual resources, can provide the warrant or give the assurance that one shall remain faithful to God.

Our inability to safeguard our relationship to God is, however, the human side of a wonderful security. The fact is that there is no area of life that can be so secure, so protected against loss, as our oneness with God. That is the message of the seventh chapter of Revelation. The security that Revelation talks about differs from all other security in one basic respect. It is not a security which *we* obtain, which *we* achieve, or which *we* create. It is a security which *God* gives. It is *He* who seals His people. It is *He* who surrounds them with a protection that can never be broken. That is the meaning of the sealing of the 144,000.

The sealing of the servants of God was a protection against persecution and against the power of the persecuting Roman empire. But this must be correctly understood. God did not promise that Christians would not be persecuted. He did not promise that they would not suffer from the judgments that would fall on the entire empire. He did not secure them against persecuting and judging events. He secured them against the power of these events to harm or break their relationship to God. He promised them this:

> . . . neither death, nor life, nor angels, nor
> principalities, nor things present, nor things to come,
> nor powers, nor height, nor depth,
> nor anything else in all creation,
> will be able to separate us
> from the love of God in Christ Jesus our Lord.

(Romans 8:38,39)

This is a promise given to a Church under the whip of persecution. Any body of Christians which is harassed or opposed or denied the right of existence may draw great comfort from it. In many countries where the Church is established it does not have to suffer any outward persecution. On the contrary, the right of freedom of worship is written into many constitutions and is protected by law. It would be a great mistake, however, to think that in such world areas the servants of God do not need to be sealed against spiritual harm. Indeed, they may need the sealing even more than believers in a persecuted Church.

It has been the experience of the Church throughout the ages that when it does not suffer from external danger,

danger to its spiritual health arises from within. God gave comforting promises to John in the light of the dangers that the Church was facing at that time. Today the dangers facing the Church in many world areas are of quite a different kind. When the Church does not suffer from persecution, it may suffer from the even greater dangers of outward security, riches, pride, or spiritual indifference. It may, like the church of Laodicea, think that it is rich and needs nothing, whereas in fact it may be wretched, pitiable, poor, blind, and naked (3:17). Against such threats to its life the Church needs sealing no less than against dangers that come to it from the outside. The beast of empire against which the early Church struggled can also appear in the sheep's clothing of false messiahs, of wealth, of harmful teachings, of alliances with the state or business or other powers in society which lead the Church to become a fearful and calculating witness to the truth.

The sealing of the 144,000 is a promise of God's protection of the soundness and health of the believer's love of God and trust in His power. The gates of hell shall not prevail against the Church. The gates of fiery persecuting enemies shall not prevail against it. But, equally, the gates of attractive, cultured, prosperous, tempting ease and comfort in the world shall not conquer it either.

THE SEVEN TRUMPETS

Chapters 8 and 9

Up to this point the explanation of the imagery in Revelation has, in spite of difficulties, been fairly simple. The remainder of the book is more difficult to grasp. The language becomes even more symbolic than it has been. How shall we enter into the meaning of figures such as locusts that look like horses, wear crowns of gold, have human faces, women's hair, teeth like lions' teeth, armour like iron scales, and tails that sting like scorpions? Through the centuries students of the Scriptures have concerned themselves with these difficulties and have shed light on them. We continue our study, therefore, in the confidence that Revelation was meant for the Church of all time, and that they who read the book and keep what is written in it will be blessed.

1   The silence of one half hour, verses 1,2

The breaking of the seals in Chapter 6 brought us to the point of the final judgment. It did not, however, describe that judgment itself. That, as we shall see, comes later in the book. It brought us to the end of one cycle of description of God's dealings with the world. The seventh seal begins a second cycle. It does not have an independent content as the previous six seals had. Instead, the seventh seal is the mother of seven new judgments. These are the judgments announced by the seven trumpet-blowing angels. So awesome and dreadful are these judgments going to be that when the seal that introduces them is opened, there is silence in heaven for half an hour.

Silence is often an expression of reverence and awe. It

may signify a waiting with anxious concern for the disclosure of some great matter, whether human or divine. That is the kind of silence we find in this chapter. When the seventh seal is broken, heaven's inhabitants are so overcome by its meaning that they are silent for half an hour. The prolonged silence indicates that what we are about to see will be wholly awesome.

John now sees 'the seven angels who stand before God' and each of them receives a trumpet. The words 'the seven angels' instead of simply 'seven angels' means that they are known, familiar angels. In all probability they refer to 'the seven angels of the presence' (i.e. of God), well-known to John's readers from the apocryphal literature but hardly known to Bible readers today.

2 The prayers of the saints, verses 3-5

Another angel whose task is closely related to the seven trumpet blowers now appears and takes his stand before the altar. In his hand he has a golden censer. The function of a censer in Israel's worship was to carry live coals for burning incense in the temple. The ascending smoke had a fragrant smell which was well-pleasing to God. On the great Day of Atonement the censer was used to produce a cloud of sweet fragrance in the Holy of Holies above the ark (Leviticus 16:12-13). In time incense became a symbol of acceptable prayer (Psalm 141:2; Luke 1:10). The prayers that are sent to God from this altar are not the same as the cries of the souls under the altar in Revelation 6:9-11. In 8:3-5 the prayers that are offered are 'the prayers of all the saints', that is, all God's people who are on the earth at any given time. It may be assumed, however, in view of what follows, that these prayers are similar to the cries described in 6:9-11.

The prayers of all the saints not only please God but they have a surprising second effect. When the angel takes fire off the altar from which the incense ascended, he casts it on the earth. He does this with the same censer that offered the incense to God. When this fire strikes the earth, it causes peals of thunder, loud noises, flashes of lightning, and an earthquake. After this, the seven angels blow the seven trumpets of judgment that shall afflict the earth. The message of this symbolism is that the petitions for justice made by God's people bring down judgment upon the world. Although the souls under the altar must wait until the End for the final judgment of God, there are preliminary judgments in response to the prayers of all the saints.

3   The first four trumpets, verses 6-13

Revelation is a book with a message about something because it is first of all a book that *points* to something. We can understand what it says only when we know what it points to. In Revelation angels, as we have noted before, represent first and foremost the power, working, and authority of God. In chapters 8 and 9 it is especially necessary to remember that the power of God in the world usually does not express itself directly but *indirectly*. When the second commandment says that God will punish the iniquity of the fathers upon the children to the third and fourth generation of those who hate Him (Exodus 20:4-6), we have an illustration of this divine law. The idolatry of the fathers with all the sins associated with it creates a morally and spiritually sick society which falls apart under its own sin. The law, 'As you sow so shall you reap', holds not only for individuals, but also for whole societies, nations, indeed for mankind as a whole. God has so created man that his actions carry within themselves their own reward of blessing or their own penalty of punishment. Such scriptural statements as, 'he who takes the sword shall perish by the sword'; 'the measure you give will be the measure you get back'; 'figs are not gathered from thorns'; 'to him who has shall be given, and from him who has not shall be taken even that which he has', are illustrations of this principle. These are not descriptions of external punishments and rewards. They are descriptions of the functioning of our human nature as God made it. When these laws work out in life, we see what is meant by the warning that God is not mocked. The understanding of this principle is basic to the understanding of the judgments announced by the trumpets.

The seven angels are divided into two groups. The first four, which are dealt with in this part, announce judgments on the physical world. The last three announce judgments on men. At the same time, the seven judgments constitute a united and interrelated whole.

The first judgment falls on the earth (the land mass), verse 7; the second falls on seas and oceans (salt water bodies), verses 8, 9; the third falls on rivers and lakes and on their sources (sweet water bodies), verses 10,11; the fourth affects the light-bearers (sun, moon, and stars), verse 12.

In each case, a third of their power is destroyed; a third of trees and vegetation is burned up; a third of the oceans becomes blood so that life cannot exist in them; a third of all ships on the seas are destroyed; a third of all fresh water becomes bitter so that it cannot be drunk and men die of thirst; and a third of the light is darkened.

Let us see what the picture means up to this point.

a. There is no part of the world or of the universe that is beyond the reach of God's judging power. Land, sea, rivers, heavenly bodies—all are in His hand.

b. Although these judgments fall on physical aspects of the world, they are intended to punish men. When trees and vegetation are burned up, when fish die in huge quantities, when storms destroy ships, when fresh water is poisoned so that it cannot be drunk, and when the light of nature is darkened, then obviously human beings are very directly affected.

c. The judgments are not total. They affect a part, a large part, a third of the physical world. Their partial character indicates their purpose. They are intended to lead men to repent of their sin. This is not stated directly with respect to the first four judgments; it is clearly implied with respect to the last three: 'the rest of mankind . . . did not repent of the works of their hands . . . nor did they repent of their murders or their sorceries or their immorality or their thefts' (9:21). At the same time, there is a progression in severity in the second cycle of judgments. In the judgment of the fourth seal Death and Hades received power over one fourth of the earth. In five of the trumpet judgments this is increased to one third.

d. The prophetic value of the judgments here described is large indeed. They have a meaning far greater than anything that John could have known or understood. We touch here on the whole problem of ecology, which is of such profound concern for the world of our time. The judgments announced by the first four trumpets have to do with the poisoning or destruction of our natural world-home. They affect the land, forests, fields, seas, rivers, lakes, and their inhabitants—insects, fish, birds, animals, and men.

The destruction of our world-home, so far as our experience and observation of it are concerned, takes place in two ways. The first is the destruction which nature itself effects; the second is that which man effects. An example of the former is the Sahara Desert. When Europe was in its Ice Age, about twenty thousand years ago, and when earth's population was small, the area now called the Sahara was a moist, warm, temperate land. It was drained by a river system and consisted mainly of grassland or, as it is more commonly called, savannah. The same kinds of land areas are called prairies in North America, pampas in South America, steppes in Russia, and veldts in South Africa. When the Ice Age came to an end and the rains stopped, that area gradually dried up and became *sahara*, the Arabic word for desert.

The second kind of destruction is inflicted by man. He has engaged in this from the beginning of history. At first he did so in small ways and only locally, such as poisoning wells, covering enemy farmlands with stones, or burning forests and crops. As population increased and tools and weapons became more refined, he did so on an ever larger scale. Such action could and did affect bird and animal life, climate and rainfall, soil erosion, and various occupations of men.

These did not become a serious world problem, however, until the present century. By introducing machinery into manufacture and travel in the nineteenth century, we have created huge dangers for mankind. The nature, the world-home, that was meant to be man's servant, his friend, and the supplier of his physical needs, has in many places been turned into a deadly enemy. Nature did not turn itself into an enemy. Man did this. Man the exploiter did not realize that as a seeing, breathing, eating, earth-related creature he is himself a part of the nature that surrounds him. He did not understand that what hurts nature also hurts him.

We have exploited the natural world. We have robbed it, abused it, and especially we have used it as a global cesspool. Into its rivers the most 'advanced' societies, the so-called 'developed' countries, have discharged all the dirt of their cities, factories, and homes. Into its lakes and seas and oceans Western man has unloaded all the waste of his ships. Into its air he has emitted all the smoke of his factories, trains, lorries, and aeroplanes. His wars have made the whole world a battle-field. No region, no country, is safe from nuclear bombs that can utterly destroy whole cities. In Vietnam huge areas of forest and vegetation have been defoliated by spraying poison, from aeroplanes.

It may be difficult in Africa or Asia to suppose that the sun could lose a third of its light. But anyone who has visited European or American manufacturing centres knows that a haze of smoke can dim the landscape for miles around. In Los Angeles this haze is called smog because it is a combination of man-created smoke (chiefly emissions from cars) and natural fog. In some areas one can look full into the sun on a cloudless day and experience no pain of eye because the thick layer of factory smoke completely dulls the brightness of the sun. Serious efforts are now being made to clean the air and the water, but it is a question whether in many world areas it is not already too late.

When one reads 8:6-12 in the light of these developments, the picture drawn for us in Revelation will not seem strange or absurd. The bitterness of it all is that these calamities are wholly of man's own making. The threat to continued existence of life on the earth is self-made by man. Paul's words are true:

> . . . the wisdom of this world is folly with God. For it is written, 'He catches the wise in their craftiness,' and again, 'The Lord knows that the thoughts of the wise are futile.' So let no one boast of men.
>
> (1 Corinthians 3: 19-21)

But how many see the judgment of God in these things? They are all attributed to human errors, miscalculation, lack of foresight and planning. Always, too, men comfort themselves that they have the ability to correct their mistakes and shortcomings. They can still usher in the Golden Age of Man. This is not the repentance that God looks for, nor is it the attitude that works reconciliation with him.

4 The fifth trumpet, 8:13-9:11

An eagle now mounts to mid-heaven and cries that three more judgments are to come. These will not be directed against the earth and its resources but against men. Three times over he cries out 'Woe!' to those who dwell on the earth. Woe is a description of distinctively human suffering.

When the fifth angel blows his trumpet, John sees a star on the earth that has fallen from heaven. This star is an angel. The ancient world believed that stars were angels. In the Bible good angels always descend or appear, i.e. they manifest themselves in a graceful, dignified manner. Evil angels, on the other hand, are cast out or fall from heaven. The angel which John sees on the earth is not identified. He is probably Abaddon or Apollyon, mentioned in verse 11. To this angel is given the key to the bottomless pit. He does not therefore have authority or power over it himself. He has power over the pit only so long as he possesses the key to it.

The pit or the abyss was a familiar idea in the religious world of John's time. It was a horrible, fear-inspiring area that had neither an earth below it nor a heaven above it. In Enoch, the best known of the apocalyptic books, rather detailed descriptions of it are given. The following passage suggests the popular view in John's time:

> And I proceeded to where things were chaotic. And there I saw something horrible: I saw neither a heaven nor a firmly founded earth, but a place chaotic and horrible. And there I saw seven stars of the heaven bound together in it, like great mountains and burning with fire . . . . These are the numbers of the stars of heaven which have transgressed the commandment of the Lord. . . . And from thence I went to another place, which was still more horrible . . . this place is the prison of the angels, and they will be imprisoned for ever.
>
> (Enoch 21)

The bottomless pit is therefore the dwelling place of disobedient angels that have been cast out of heaven. When this pit is opened, smoke arises out of it so thick and black that the light of the sun is darkened. Out of the smoke come vast numbers of demons in the form of swarms of locusts. John's description of them is largely based on Joel 1:6,7 and 2:4-7. There, however, they are destroyers of vegetation. In Revelation they are tormentors of men. Their appearance is altogether frightful. They look like ranks of cavalry ready to charge into battle. On their heads are what look like golden crowns of victory. Their faces indicate human intelligence, their hair has the soft seductiveness of a woman's tresses. Their teeth rend prey like the teeth of lions, and they are covered with armour that cannot be pierced by any weapon. Their wings give forth the frightening sound of war chariots rushing against the enemy. Somehow a scorpion's tail is united with the locust body and its sting inflicts unspeakable pain.

The effects on men are:

a. that the locust-scorpions can hurt only those who are not sealed by God;

b. they can torture such men for 'five months' but cannot kill them;

c. this torture will be so severe that men would rather die than bear it, but death flies from them when they seek it; and

d. all of this arises out of the pit or the abyss.

There are evil influences at work in the world which are not human but which express themselves notably through human means. Scripture calls them spirits, unclean spirits, evil spirits, demons. We are unable to localize the abyss or the pit out of which they come. It is external to man and the world, but man and the world are open to its inhabitants. The Bible presents demons as wanting to reside in humans or in animals. They do not like to be without some sort of body to dwell in (Matthew 12:43-45; Mark 5:1-13). Their mode of operation is totally related to the life of man and of nature. It is impossible to isolate the evil that comes out of the demonic world from the evil that man and nature themselves cause. This evil power is today often referred to collectively as 'the demonic'. Its ability to hurt, to seduce, to frighten, and the difficulty of wounding or destroying it, John sets forth in his dramatic imagery.

No one, not even devout believers, are immune to attack from the world of demons. John limits their power in two ways. The first is that they are unable to separate the believer from his Lord. He whom God has sealed may suffer from demonic attack; however, it is unable to destroy the life that God has created through faith in Christ. The second limitation is one of time. The attack of the demons will sooner or later exhaust itself. But while it lasts, it can be so severe that its victims would prefer to die. A healthy body may long continue to shelter a sick and horribly suffering mind. The leader of the demonic host is therefore properly called the Destroyer. He takes peace from the hearts of men and he destroys it among men. This is the judgment that again and again falls upon men who do not fear God, who do not know His forgiveness.

5 The sixth trumpet, 9:12-21

The judgment of the sixth trumpet affects the physical lives of men rather than their souls. A third of mankind is killed by the sixth trumpet judgment. This is what chiefly distinguishes the sixth judgment from the fifth.

When the sixth angel blows his trumpet, John hears a voice from the four horns of the altar before the throne of God. This reminds us that all the trumpet judgments are divine responses to the prayers of God's people (8:1-5). The voice authorizes the release of four angels standing at the Euphrates River. In the Old Testament the Euphrates is the dividing line between the great eastern empires of Babylonia-Assyria-Persia and the area that David governed at the height of Israel's power. For Israel, invasion came from the east. At the time John wrote, Persia was a similar danger for the Roman empire. The four angels would then represent the power of Persia as it stood ready to invade the Roman lands.

When the set time comes, the four angels send 200,000,000 cavalry against the world. The huge number simply indicates a power so vast that it is not possible to resist it. The riders and the horses on which they ride are pictured in the same kind of language used to describe the fifth trumpet judgment. Fire, smoke, and sulphur issue from their mouths. This would remind readers of the volcanic eruptions which were well known in the ancient world. The tails with which the horses wounded men seem to be an enlargement of the tails of the locust-scorpions of the fifth judgment. One third of mankind is killed by their attacks.

We saw in the fifth trumpet judgment that the tortures which the locusts inflicted were in fact the end-result of man's own sinfulness. Could the same be true here? The age of atomic power and nuclear fission has only just begun. We may date their public beginning from the explosion of two atomic bombs over the Japanese cities of Hiroshima and Nagasaki at the close of World War II. Each bomb destroyed a city and killed some fifty thousand people in the city concerned. What are the limits of destructive capacity which begins with such dreadful power? And what other capacities for human annihilation can man develop? The laboratories have already prepared poisonous gases with indescribable lethal power. The weapons known as biological warfare, through which deadly germs are let loose over a country, lies ready for use in the arsenals of the great powers. And there are the catastrophes of nature which periodically claim their tens of thousands of human lives.

When these judgments come to afflict mankind, men will not repent but rather harden themselves in their sin. Suffering can indeed be a means to lead men to God, but not by itself. Being led back to God requires hearing God speak through the suffering.

Meaning for today
Today there is a strong tendency in Christian circles to express faith and life in terms of Christian action. In literature, politics, the arts, economics, education, medicine, journalism, Christianity seeks to act as a force in society for improving the quality of thought and life. This is a needed corrective for the kind of meditative Christianity that has been so common in the past. It believed its power to be best expressed in the private life only, rather than in both the private and the public life. We are called, however, to be a power in the whole of society.

Revelation emphasizes the power of prayer but says little about direct Christian action for the influencing of society. The prayers of all the saints ascend to God and are then, as it were, cast on the earth and cause fearful judgments there. As no other book in the Bible, Revelation teaches the profound effects of prayer on the social, political, and economic orders of mankind. The effect of such prayer, however, is very different from that intended and often achieved by Christian action. The latter intends to be and often is creative and enriching. Prayer as presented in Revelation 8 and 9 is an appeal for justice. God hears these petitions of His people and in response to them rains judgments upon the earth. Moreover, the power of prayer as reflected in these chapters is very indirect. It registers complaint with God and He responds to it in His own time and way. When He does, He responds to it in a manner so natural, so closely related to man's sinful action and its results, that it is hardly recognizable as an answer to prayer.

When we speak of prayer in this connection, we must take the word in a very broad sense. It refers not only to articulate spoken prayer by individuals and groups. It has in mind no less the suffering, the anguish, the crying out of God's people. A strong instance of this is the oppression suffered by the Israelites in Egypt.

> And the people of Israel groaned under their bondage, and cried out for help, and their cry under bondage came up to God . . . and God saw the people of Israel, and God knew their condition.
>
> (Exodus 2:23-25)

God's judgments are further obscured to the believer because they strike the believing as well as the unbelieving community. The New Testament Church is not, like Israel in Egypt, resident in a separate province which is protected against the judgments that fall on the world as a whole. Indeed, often it deserves and receives judgment itself. Believers are protected spiritually against the judgments of God but not in other ways. War, famine, pestilence, earthquakes, economic disasters, social unrest affect the Christian and the non-Christian alike. But where the one curses God and hardens his heart, the other acknowledges the righteousness of God and bows his head under the chastisement. In the loss of comforts and goods he becomes richer in Christ and in grace.

As a book of comfort for Christians in trouble, Revelation discloses another great truth. All the forces of evil, all sin, all the demonic world, all that would harm, is under Christ's control. He does not destroy sin before the End comes. He does limit it. He sets its boundaries. What comes out of the pit of evil can do so only because He has permitted it. Its monstrous inhabitants have power only five months. Then new faces appear to destroy the old ones. When the Church flees into the wilderness and the dragon vomits out water like a river to drown her, the earth opens its mouth to receive the threat to her life (12:15,16). During the Reformation the entire movement led by Martin Luther would have been crushed overwhelmingly by the powerful Emperor Charles the Fifth if the eastern boundaries of his empire had not been constantly threatened by Muslim invasion.

Even so, the powers of evil are frightening. The more the world is drawn together by modern science and invention, the more self-contradictory its life becomes. One feels also that human perversity alone could not make human society as perverse and wicked as it is. It is at this point that we begin to sense the demonic, the dark cloud of evil beings that ascends continually out of some unholy pit to make man destroy himself. It is especially in the structures of society that the demonic uses and re-enforces the sinfulness of man. Evil powers work through exploitation, oppression, privilege, custom, manipulation, mistaken values, the struggle of class against class, tribe against tribe, nation against nation, to make society self-destructive. The successes of yesterday can become the nightmares of tomorrow. The cities of the world, where men live so closely together, are the most lonely, the most inhospitable places on earth. The great strides made in the developing countries in primary education turn into vast social problems when two-thirds of the school leavers can find no place to continue their schooling or no satisfactory place in which to work. Wars, social revolutions, economic cycles, political upheavals, changing morals, changing life-styles, the imbalance of supply and demand, the wealth of the few and the poverty of the many present unending and explosive problems to whole societies. Statesmen, financiers, scientists, military leaders, social thinkers live in fear and trembling as they seek to prevent the forces with which they deal from devouring the societies which they seek to serve. And when solutions are found, why is it that so often the solution of one problem bears in its womb two new problems bigger than the one that was overcome?

Believers are caught up in these disturbing circumstances just as much as those who do not know Christ. But there is a difference, indeed a very big difference, between them in these circumstances. The unbeliever sees no point of rest, no real security, no true stability anywhere. Everything is changing, often for the worst. He sees no hope of deliverance from a life that moves from one crisis to another, from one danger to another. The believer knows the God and Father of our Lord Jesus Christ. He knows that with him 'there is no variation or shadow due to change' (James 1:17). He is the Creator, He sets the boundaries for all evil, He has already defeated and overcome it in Christ. He establishes the good. The nations are in His hand. The Anointed One of God has been given all power in heaven and on earth. The believer has seen the Almighty on His heavenly throne, surrounded by angels, redeemed men, and great majesty and power. This mighty God is more than simply there, far away in a place called heaven. He is here, He is with us, He is in us. He does not leave us to ourselves. He strengthens us with courage, faith, and hope. We believe His Word. We have a knowledge that the wise men of the earth do not have.

This is what makes the Christian a calm and stable person. His hopes and fears do not alternate between the heights of certainty and the depths of new dangers. The always changing headlines, the news reports, leadership promises, and leadership betrayals do not shake but rather deepen his hope in the promises, constancy, and faithfulness of God. Therefore he can work calmly and patiently, doing God's will, and be a rock of strength in his community and in the nation.

PREPARATION FOR POURING OUT THE SEVEN BOWLS OF GOD'S WRATH

Chapters 10 and 11

We have come to the third and last preparation for the third and last group of God's judgments. It is well to remember at this point that there are three great pairs of preparation and judgment in Revelation. The first deals with the seven seals, the second with the seven trumpets, and the third with the seven bowls of the wrath of God (or the seven last plagues). In each case the preparation has to do with the protection of God's people, the judgment with punishment of their enemies.

1 The mighty angel, 10:1-7

The angel whom John now sees has all the characteristics of might and power that we have noted before: a rainbow over his head, a face bright-shining as the sun, powerful legs appearing like pillars of fire. What is new in the description of the angel is the expression 'wrapped in a cloud'. Clouds are often associated in the Bible with things that are heavenly: God's power in nature (Psalm 104:3), the second coming of our Lord (Mark 13:16), the ascent of the saints to heaven (1 Thessalonians 4:17). The cloud therefore suggests heavenly origin and contributes to the majesty of the angel's appearance. He has in his hands a little scroll which differs from the scroll in Revelation 4 and 5 in that it is not sealed but open. The opening of the first scroll by the Lamb revealed the secrets that were in it. Here the message is clear. The scroll is given open.

The great angel claims universal authority. He sets one foot on land and one foot on the sea. He cries out with a loud voice like a lion roaring, and when he has done so, the 'seven thunders sounded'. What the seven thunders said was understood by John, for he was about to write their message down. But a voice from heaven instructed him not to do so. What John heard was not to be revealed. The seven thunders were for John what the things that Paul saw in the third heaven were for him. He heard 'things that cannot be told, which man may not utter' (2 Corinthians 12:4). They suggest that there are dimensions of reality which man is not able in this life to contemplate.

The angel lifts up his right hand to heaven and swears with a mighty oath that the end is near. There will be delay no longer. When the seventh trumpet shall sound, the purposes of God will have been realized, the mystery of His plan shall stand fully revealed, and the End shall come. The thought is similar to Paul's writing that now we see in a mirror dimly but then face to face (1 Corinthians 13:12). The mystery of God shall have been fulfilled when the effects of the seventh trumpet blast have worked themselves out in the world.

The expression 'no more delay', however, does not mean the immediate introduction of the End. It means that there will be no more *delay*, that is to say, there will be no unnecessary waiting, no following of paths that lead nowhere. 'For yet a little while, and the coming one shall come and shall not tarry' (Hebrews 10:37). There remains therefore that 'little while', the length of which or short-ness of which is determined by Him for whom one day is as a thousand years and a thousand years as one day (2 Peter 3:8). This 'little while', this waiting which is not delaying, is related to the little scroll which is open in the hands of the angel.

2 The little scroll, 10:8-11

The heavenly voice which had earlier spoken to John now speaks to him again. He must 'take the scroll which is open in the hand of the angel who is standing on the sea and on the land'. When John has done so, the angel says to him, 'Take it and eat; it will be bitter in your stomach but sweet as honey in your mouth.' Since eating and tasting precede digestion, the order of words here is peculiar. In the next verse, however, the order is as we would expect it to be. What is the meaning of this symbol?

The figure of a scroll that is to be eaten is drawn from Ezekiel 2:8-3:3. Here Ezekiel is told, 'Son of man, . . . eat this scroll. . . . I ate it, and it was in my mouth sweet as honey.' There is no indication of its bitterness in his stomach, but there can be little doubt about the fact of the matter. The writing on the scroll was 'words of lamentation and mourning and woe' (2:10), so that when he went to preach them he did so 'in bitterness in the heat of my spirit' (3:14). To be made a steward of the mysteries of God is indeed a wonderful thing, 'sweet as honey in the mouth', but the exercise of that stewardship always brings a double response—one of acceptance and one of rejection. Paul was profoundly aware of this double response to the gospel:

> For we are the aroma of Christ to God among those who are being saved and among those who are perishing, to one a fragrance from death to death, to the other a fragrance from life to life. Who is sufficient for these things?

(2 Corinthians 2:15,16)

It is with this background in mind that John hears the words, 'You must again prophesy about many peoples and nations and tongues and kings.'

Several matters should be noted in connection with the instruction which John received. The first is that the command to preach was obviously not given to him simply as an individual. It was given to him as the bearer of Christ's message to the seven churches, i.e. the Church in its entirety (Revelation 1:11). The preaching must therefore be done by the Church. The second is that the message which must be preached is the same as that which must be preached by the two witnesses in chapter 11, as we shall observe later. Third, it seems strange that the Church must preach 'about many peoples, nations, tongues, and kings'. The gospel is not about the nations and their rulers. It is about the redemptive work of Christ. The preaching of the gospel, however, has meaning for tribes and nations and rulers as well as for individuals. The command of Christ to preach the gospel requires the Church to make disciples of all nations (Matthew 28:19), even though only individuals can believe and be baptized. The reason for the persecution which the Roman empire launched against the Church is precisely the fact that the preaching of the Church soon affected all the structures of Roman society.

3 The measuring of the temple, 11:1,2a

The symbol of the measuring of 'the temple of God and the altar and those who worship there' has the same meaning as the sealing of the 144,000. The picture of the measuring is drawn in the first instance from Amos 7:7. There the Lord tells Amos to measure Israel. The purpose of the measuring is to indicate what is to be destroyed and what is to be preserved. Given over to destruction were 'the high places of Israel . . . the sanctuaries of Israel . . . and the house of Jeroboam.' In the case of the temple which John is to measure, the picture is somewhat different. Here the measuring indicates not what is to be destroyed but what is to be saved from destruction. Only the most central and sacred part of the temple is to be measured: the Holy of Holies, the holy place, the altar and those who worship there (i.e. the priests) are to be measured and are thereby protected. That is to say, they are set apart, withdrawn, from the impending destruction. These two areas, the priests and the altar of incense (symbolizing the prayers of God's people), represent all the servants of God.

A striking illustration of measuring as an act of protection is found in the apocryphal book of Enoch, chapter 61:1-5. 'And I saw in those days how cords were given to those angels . . . and they went to the north. And I asked the angels, saying unto him, "Why have those angels taken those cords and gone off?" And he said unto me, "They have gone to measure." And the angel said unto me: "These shall bring the measures of the righteous . . . that they may return and stay themselves on the day of the Elect One; for none shall be destroyed before the Lord of the spirits, and none can be destroyed".'

The court of the Gentiles, which was separated from these areas in Herod's temple, will suffer the same fate in the coming destruction as the holy city. Both will be trampled by unbelieving nations for a period of forty-two months. This indicates that the Church will suffer persecution but that the extent of the persecution will be limited. The meaning of the expression 'forty-two months' and its significance in the book as a whole makes it desirable to devote a separate discussion to that subject.

4 The forty-two months, 11:2b

This expression does not stand by itself in Revelation. It refers to the same period of time indicated by the 'one thousand two hundred and sixty days' (42 months × 30 days) during which the witnesses preach (11:3) and the 'time, two times and a half time' (1 year + 2 years + ½ year) of Revelation 12:14. To understand the meaning of these figures it is necessary to refer to the exile of the Jews of Babylon and to their later history. The exile dates from 586 B.C. to the return of the Jews in 538 under Cyrus and on later occasions. Palestine remained under Persian rule for nearly two hundred years after Cyrus conquered Babylon in 539. The years 333 to 323 B.C. saw the rise and conquests of Alexander the Great, the Macedonian king. He conquered Persia, as also Egypt, and with these conquests Palestine also came under his rule. When he died in 323 B.C. his huge empire was divided among four generals. Of these, two are significant for our present discussion. Seleucis received Syria and areas north and east of it; Ptolemy received Egypt and its surrounding areas, including Palestine. In the wars between Egypt and Syria that followed, Syria gained control of Palestine in 198 B.C. Under the Ptolemys the Jews had enjoyed religious freedom. This they lost when the Seleucids gained control of their country. It was their policy to enforce Greek culture and religion on their subjects.

The greatest trial of the Jews came in the reign of Antiochus IV, 175-163 B.C. In December 168 B.C. he desecrated Jewish holy places, offered swine on the temple altar, erected an image in the temple, and introduced prostitutes into it. Under the leadership of seven brothers called the Maccabees the Jews revolted and gained their freedom. The period from the first desecration of the temple to the restoration of worship in it was traditionally believed to be three and a half years. These three and a half years of war and suffering made such an impression on the Jews that they became for them a symbol of the troubled time which, they believed, would precede the End of all things. This figure John adopted as his own. In Revelation it is called forty-two months, one thousand two hundred and sixty days, and a time, two times, and a half time. Three and a half years is the language of ordinary history; the other references, as we shall see, are made in the mysterious language of apocalyptic writing.

5 The two witnesses, 11:3-14

In Revelation 10:11 John, representing the Church in its entirety, is told 'You must again prophesy about many peoples and nations and tongues and kings.' That is the task that is now to be carried out by the two witnesses. They prophesy one thousand two hundred and sixty days. This is the same length as forty-two months, and in the history which we are tracing, it covers exactly the same period of time. In chapter 12 it becomes clear that the time in these two references is the period of the Church extending from the first coming of Christ to His return. But why are the two different expressions used?

In both 11:2 and 13:5 the forty-two months refer to a time of conquest, victory, and domination. Such a time always appears to pass rapidly. The witnessing is done in sackcloth (11:3), the dress of grief and sorrow. The refuge in the wilderness (12:5) bears the same character. Such time always appears to pass slowly. Therefore the same period bears two names: forty-two months from the viewpoint of the victorious enemy, and one thousand two hundred and sixty days from the viewpoint of the suffering Church. The time duration on the calendar is the same, but the appearance of psychological experience of the one is short, that of the other long.

The witnesses are two. Perhaps this is a reference to the biblical principle that in the mouth of two witnesses every word shall be established (Deuteronomy 19:15, Matthew 18:16).

Who are these witnesses? They are described as two olive trees and two lampstands. That this is four in all does not bother the apocalyptic writer. Two twos is the same as two. The lampstand, as we have seen, is a picture of the Church. The olive tree, clearly drawn from Zechariah 4, provides the oil that is symbolic of the power of the Holy Spirit, who gives light and understanding to the Church. It is in this chapter that the well-known words are found, 'Not by might, nor by power, but by my Spirit, says the Lord' (Zechariah 4:6).

That the witnesses are the Church or believers as a whole (the 144,000) is further shown in the power which they have. They can consume their foes and have power to prevent rain, to turn water into blood, and to send plagues on the earth when they desire. Elijah and Moses are doubtless in mind here. At the transfiguration of Jesus they represented the Old Testament people of God. Here the witnesses are a symbol of the New Testament Church. The language sounds strange in New Testament ears. When and where does or did the Church invoke plagues on her enemies? The strangeness of language disappears when we remember how God responds to the prayers of His persecuted people (Revelation 8 and 9). When a blinding flash of light cast Saul from his horse on his way to Damascus to arrest Christians there, he heard the words, 'Saul, Saul, why do you persecute me?' (Acts 9:4). How many prayers in Jerusalem and in Damascus lay behind this incident? To attack the Church of Christ is to invite self-destruction. Saul repented and became the incomparable Paul, but far more often judgment leads to greater rebellion and greater judgment (9:20,21).

When the witnesses have finished their testimony, a beast emerges from the bottomless pit and kills them. We shall discuss 'the beast' when we study Revelation 13. At this point we shall only note that when the period given for preaching does not lead to repentance, the world, burdened by a hardened conscience, will kill the witnesses, and their dead bodies will lie unburied. Or they may shut them up in prison or send them into exile or otherwise deprive them of place and position in society. There are many ways to kill the witness of the gospel.

At this point Jerusalem suddenly becomes 'Sodom and Egypt', where the Lord of the witnesses was crucified. The holy city now becomes the world-city, organizing all its powers to resist God. It is the Christ-crucifying city, fixing a mocking sign at the top of the cross, 'Jesus of Nazareth, the King of the Jews' in the language of Jewish religion (Hebrew), Hellenic wisdom (Greek), and Roman power (Latin) (John 19:20). And there is great rejoicing that the tormentors are out of the way.

The joy is of short duration. It lasts only three and a half days, a mere fragment of time compared to the 1260 days extending from the first to the second coming of our Lord. Then the End comes. The dead in Christ will rise and those believers who are still alive will be transformed and be taken to meet the Lord in the air together with their resurrected brethren (1 Thessalonians 4:16,17; 1 Corinthians 15:51,52). Meanwhile, the disintegration of the world-city begins and men do homage to God not because of repentance, but because of fear, as in Revelation 6:15-17.

The description of the End is very incomplete. Much is left unsaid. There is still a third series of woes to come. The seven last plagues to be announced by the seventh trumpet have yet to be poured out. Then will come the full, the final, End of all things, and with it the initiation of the new heaven and the new earth that shall endure for ever.

6 The seventh trumpet, 11:15-19

When the seventh trumpet blows, we are surprised that no judgments are announced. After the first four trumpets had been blown, an eagle flying in mid-heaven had cried with a loud voice, 'Woe, woe, woe to those who dwell on the earth, at the blasts of the other trumpets which the three angels are about to blow' (8:13). When the first one had blown, John wrote, 'The first woe has passed; behold two woes are still to come' (9:12). When the second angel had blown he wrote, 'The second woe has passed; behold the third woe is soon to come' (11:14). Now the last trumpet blows but not a judgment is announced. Instead, 'there were loud voices in heaven; saying; "The kingdom of the world has become the kingdom of our Lord and of his Christ, and he shall reign for ever and ever".' Thereupon the twenty-four elders praise God, God's temple is opened in heaven, there are impressive events of nature on the earth, and that is all. No woes are announced. This requires explanation. Indeed, there are several problems of interpretation here which must be faced before we can fruitfully go on to the following chapters.

The absence of woes in the blowing of the seventh trumpet is one problem. Another is the statement in verse 14, 'The second woe has passed, behold the third woe is soon to come.' This leaves the impression that the ascent of the two witnesses and the earthquake in the city (verses 12, 13) marked the end of the second woe (the sixth trumpet). But this clearly cannot be the case. The third problem is that the flashes of lightning, loud noises, the peals of thunder, a great earthquake, the disintegration of the city, and the falling of great hailstones, all of which are mentioned in 11:13 and 11:19, are again reported in 16:20. These difficulties we must try to clarify.

When the first four trumpets had been blown, three more woes were announced, as we have seen. Two of these are described in chapter 9. It is evident that both of the judgments which the fifth and sixth trumpets introduced were completed. Not only were their results summarized in 9:20,21, but according to 10:7 the third trumpet remains to be sounded, and when it is, the mystery of God will be fulfilled. For these reasons, the words in 11:14 that the second woe has passed, seem to be out of place. There are two ways in which this peculiarity may be explained. One is that in the course of the early centuries a copyist transferred the words found in 11:14 from the end of chapter 9 to its present position. Another, and perhaps more likely, possibility is that, like 9:12, it was intended to serve as an introduction to the blowing of the next trumpet. In 11:15 the last trumpet is indeed blown. But this still leaves the fact that the words, 'the second woe passed' refer to 9:13-21, not to chapters 10 and 11.

Even stranger is the absence of any woes in 11:15-19. Many interpreters consider the lightning, noises, thunder, etc. to be the woes announced by the seventh angel. But that is not possible. We find nearly the same series of natural occurrences mentioned in 4:5, 8:5, and 16:18. All of them indicate earthly responses in nature to divine actions in heaven. Moreover, if the lightning, voices, noises, etc. were the fulfilling of the mystery of God (10:7), what then is the meaning of 15:1? There we read, 'Then I saw . . . seven angels with seven plagues, which are the last, for with them the wrath of God is ended.' And what would be the meaning of the voice that followed the pouring out of the last plague (16:17), saying 'It is done'?

What we have before us in Revelation 11:14-19 would appear to be this: the seventh trumpet is blown but its contents are not immediately announced. Instead, the writer hastens to tell us of the victory which the seventh trumpet achieves: 'The kingdom of the world has become the kingdom of our Lord and of his Christ, and he shall reign for ever and ever' (11:15). The contents of the seventh trumpet are the seven last plagues. These are described in chapters 15 and 16. What is the reason for the delay in disclosing the contents of the seventh trumpet? Three lengthy chapters—12, 13, and 14—intervene between the preliminary announcements of the total victory achieved by the seventh trumpet and the disclosure of its contents. This is the Interruption of which we spoke at the beginning of the present section. What is the relationship of the Interruption to the preceding and following chapters? This is a question of fundamental importance for the understanding of Revelation as a whole and we shall take it up in the following section.

Meaning for today

One of the most comforting teachings of Revelation is the sealing or the measuring of the people of God in their afflictions. If this teaching is not correctly understood, however, our view of it can become utterly misleading and destructive. We have noted that the protection of God's people given in their being sealed or being measured applies *only* to their spiritual life. It has meaning only for the Father-child relationship existing between them and God. In that respect they enjoy a full and complete security. They need not fear. No one is able to snatch them out of Christ's hand; no one is able to snatch them out of the Father's hand (John 10:28,29). They are safe.

But life is more than a spiritual experience. We live in the body. Food, clothing, houses, schooling, liberty, fellowship, jobs, income, amenities, health, peaceful existence, law and order in society, prosperity in our undertakings, justice in the courts, the privacy of our homes, freedom to worship—all of these mean a great deal to us. Wars have been fought to protect these rights and privileges. We must understand, however, that the protection promised us in being sealed and measured does not apply to a single one of these very necessary or very desirable things. In the spiritual warfare to which we are called, every one of them is expendable. That is to say, every one of them may have to be sacrificed to the enemy. Every one, even life itself, may be lost in the performance of our service in God's kingdom and in our growth to Christian maturity. No Christian is more protected than the apostle Paul, who on his last missionary journey went to Jerusalem knowing full well that imprisonment and affliction awaited him there. This did not deter him:

> And now, behold, I am going to Jerusalem, bound in the Spirit, not knowing what shall befall me there except that the Holy Spirit testifies to me in every city that imprisonment and afflictions await me. But I do not count my life of any value or as precious to myself, if only I may accomplish my course and the ministry which I received from the Lord Jesus, to testify to the gospel of the grace of God. (Acts 20:22-24)

The eleventh chapter of Revelation sets this truth very plainly in the foreground. The two witnesses (the Church) fulfill their witnessing task. They perform it in the presence of and address it to men who hate them and to whom they are a torment. When the task is done and God's purposes have been achieved through them, then the beast that ascends out of the bottomless pit makes war on them, conquers them, and kills them. Their dead bodies lie unattended on the streets of the great city for all men to see. Yet they were men who were sealed. They were worshippers in the temple that had been measured. They were those who had been marked on their foreheads. Nothing could harm them. Christ suffered for us, and the servant is not greater than his Lord. Jesus put the matter in a very strange and striking manner:

> Nation will rise against nation . . . there will be . . . earthquakes . . . famines . . . pestilences . . . terrors and great signs from heaven. But before all this they will lay their hands on you and persecute you . . . you will be delivered up even by parents and brothers and kinsmen and friends, and some of you they will put to death. . . . But not a hair on your head will perish. (Luke 21:10-19)

This is remarkable language. You will live in the midst of wars, pestilences, and fearful signs from heaven. You will be arrested. Those closest to you will betray you. Some of you will be killed. But do not worry. Though you lose everything, do not be anxious. You will not lose one hair of your head. Not a single one. Though your tormentors tear the hair out of your head, though they put a bullet through your brains so that your hair becomes a bloody mass—*not a hair of your head will perish.*

Obviously, this is figurative language. The point is that our enemies will not be able to touch our relationship to God with even the tips of their fingers. The things that really count for us are totally secure in the hand of God.

THE GREAT ANTAGONISTS

Chapters 12, 13, 14

We now come to three chapters which I have called an Interruption. They do indeed seriously interrupt the flow of Revelation as we have followed it up to this point. After the opening vision in Revelation 1 and the letters to the seven churches in chapters 2 and 3, the book follows a clear and very methodical pattern from chapter 4 through chapter 16. It is broken only by the present unit of three chapters. The pattern, as we have seen, is: first preparation (chapters 4, 5) and first series of judgments (chapter 6); second preparation (chapter 7) and second series of judgments (chapters 8, 9); third preparation (chapters 10, 11, followed by the Interruption, chapters 12, 13, 14) and third series of judgments (chapters 15, 16).

Why is the last pair of preparation-judgments broken by an Interruption? Why does not the last series of judgments follow directly after the preparation that precedes them as in the two earlier pairs? This is an important question for understanding the structure of the book and even more for understanding the message of the book.

Up to the point at which we have now arrived several things have become clear:

1. The Church suffers persecution because of her faith.

2. The world suffers God's judgments because it persecutes His people.

3. The Church, as part of the world, suffers along with the world in these judgments.

4. Neither the persecutions nor the judgments can harm the Church's relationship to her Lord.

5. The visions of Revelation reveal that God is World Ruler. All power is in His hand. The Church's enemies cannot advance one inch beyond the boundary set by God

or one hour beyond the time that He has determined for them.

Some other matters, however, have not yet become clear. They touch questions which are in the mind of the reader but which have so far not been answered. Who or what is the persecuting power? What are the deeper backgrounds of his hostility to the Church? What is the real reason for the persecution of the Church? Is there a persecutor behind the persecutions?

These questions could doubtless have been answered earlier. But John did not choose to do this. He does not identify the persecuting power until he has fully shown the magnitude both of the conflict and of the danger that confronts the Church. Having now come to the last series of judgments, he is ready to reveal the full might, dominion, and intent of the powers of evil. These powers are: the dragon who comes down from heaven, the beast that comes up out of the sea, and the beast that comes out of the earth. But he also reveals the powers that represent the good. They are a woman standing on the moon and clothed with the sun, and a child who stands so completely under the protection of God that he is caught up to his throne.

With this double revelation the deepest backgrounds of the conflict are given. The reason for the struggle lies in heaven. From there it moves to earth, and it is on the earth that it runs the course of its history. This history we must now trace.

1 The woman, her child, and the dragon, 12:1-6

As the vision begins, John sees a woman appearing in the heavens. Her appearance is wholly majestic. She is adorned with the sun as clothing. She stands on the moon as a symbol of her sovereignty. Stars form her crown (diadem) of victory. Nevertheless, the beauty and dignity of her person cannot hide the agony which she is experiencing. She is in birth-pangs to deliver a child. She is the Old Testament community of the faithful which climaxes in the motherhood of Mary. From that community and through that personal mother, Jesus the Messiah is born. After His earthly ministry is ended, the community enlarges to become the Church of the New Testament. The Church is at the same time mother and offspring, begetter and begotten. Therefore John can speak of the later Church as the offspring of the earlier. Her agony does not cease with the birth of Christ, for she is always giving birth to new descendants. Nevertheless, the adornments of sun, moon, and stars testify to her cosmic significance. Her suffering on earth obscures a majesty that will be revealed in its time. Even now the eye of faith can see that she is seated with Christ in heavenly places (Ephesians 2:6).

Immediately after seeing the sign of the woman, John sees the no less mysterious symbol of a great red dragon. In verse 9 he is identified as 'that ancient serpent who is called the Devil and Satan'. The name Devil (in Greek *diabolos*) is the translation of the Hebrew word *shatan*, meaning accuser, adversary. In the Old Testament Satan is a mysterious figure whose actual character is not wholly clear. It is in the apocryphal literature and especially in the New Testament that he emerges as the embodiment of evil, the great opponent of God, of His creation, and of Christ. It is only in Revelation that he is called 'dragon', meaning serpent. In verse 9 he is called 'that ancient serpent . . . the deceiver of the whole world.' The reference here is doubtless to the deceiving serpent in the garden of Eden. He is the evil spirit variously referred to in the New Testament as the tempter, the evil one, Belial, Beelzebub, the ruler of this world, the accuser, the prince of demons.

John uses the ancient serpent figure of this evil power to symbolize the Devil, the arch-enemy of Christ and of His Church. He has seven heads, ten horns, and seven crowns. The seven heads indicate his great intelligence, which is supported by a fulness of power and might symbolized by the ten horns. All of this is crowned with seven diadems (crowns) which speak of his victorious and authoritative character. This fearsome, terrifying creature stretches its serpentine body throughout the sky and sweeps one third of the stars from their places and casts them on the earth. Since the ancient world conceived of the stars as spirits, the dragon is represented as bringing with him a mighty host of evil angels.

The dragon sees the woman, he goes to stand before her and waits to devour her child when it shall be born. He does not succeed in his purpose, for the child is caught up to God and to his throne. In these few words John spans the whole life of our Lord from His birth to His ascension to heaven. He does not speak about His life, His ministry, His resurrection, or of the failure of Satan to destroy Him and His work. John intends here to indicate only who the great antagonist of Christ is and the deadly character of his purpose. The woman, meanwhile, flees into the wilderness. This 'wilderness' is the world in which she must live as in an alien land. Her stay there is for the period of time already mentioned—one thousand two hundred and sixty days—the time that elapses between the first and the second coming of Christ.

2 The war in heaven, 12:7-12

Christ's ascension to heaven robs the dragon of his intended victim. But his efforts to destroy Christ are not at an end. He mounts to heaven with his host of angels and seeks to destroy his enemy there. A mighty angel bars his way with the angelic armies of heaven and utterly defeats him. They cast the dragon and his angels out of heaven so that he falls back upon the earth.

The New Testament does not explain how this battle in heaven is to be understood. Jesus said that he 'saw Satan fall like lightning from heaven' (Luke 10:18). This was probably a vision of the result of His atoning death and victorious resurrection, which was then still future. When Christ's work has been done, Satan is no longer able to accuse men before God because of their sin and guilt. Therefore it can now be said that 'the accuser of our brethren has been thrown down who accuses them day and night before God.' The salvation, power, and kingdom of God, and the authority that has been given to Christ, are now fact. They are at work in the Church. Not only has Christ conquered Satan, but Christ's followers now also conquer him in their own lives by faith in Christ's blood and by witness to His name. This rejoicing in heaven is coupled, however, with woe on the earth, for Satan knows that his time is short. Though he has been conquered, the Father of Lies continues to deceive himself most of all in hoping that he can still defeat his Conqueror.

3 The dragon, the woman, and her offspring, 12:13-17

After his defeat in heaven, Satan expresses his hostility

to Christ by harassing and persecuting His Church. In a certain sense the Church escapes the dragon's pursuit. She is given 'the two wings of the great eagle', and with these she escapes further into the wilderness. It is not possible to say who or what the 'great eagle' is. It is not necessary to understand every detail of John's symbolism. His meaning is clear enough. The Church is in the world (John 17:11), yet she is not of the world (John 17:16). Satan has no power at all over that part of her life which is not of the world. This is the part of her life that is sealed and measured. She is therefore able to flee from him. Over that aspect of her life which is in the world, he has, as we have seen, much power. Woman and offspring of the woman now merge into one. She is the people of God, known as the Church. Against the Church Satan makes continuous war. In this warfare he has two incredibly powerful allies. As the dragon contemplates how he shall further attack the Church, he stands on the shore of the sea (12:13). For it is out of the sea that the first and more powerful of these two allies will arise.

4 The beast that rises out of the sea, 13:1-10

The dragon, or Satan, does not conduct his warfare on the earth directly. He does so through two influential agents: the beast that arises out of the sea and the beast that arises out of the earth. Of these, the first beast is chief, the second is its servant.

The image of the beast that comes out of the sea is drawn from Daniel 7:1-7. In a vision Daniel sees the winds of heaven stirring up the great sea (the Mediterranean). When the word 'sea' is used symbolically in Scripture, it often means nations and peoples in their turmoil, trouble, and agitation (Psalm 65:7, Isaiah 17:12, Habakkuk 3:7-15). It has that meaning in Daniel. Out of the struggling sea of warring peoples Daniel saw four ferocious, brutal kingdoms emerge. John sees only one beast arise out of the sea. This one beast, however, is a combination of the four that Daniel saw. Like one or another of the four beasts in Daniel, it has seven heads, ten horns, ten crowns, the appearance of a leopard, feet like a bear, a mouth like a lion, and it speaks proud and blasphemous words. The one beast of John is a composite of Daniel's four. The figure that results from this mixture conveys an impression of terrible cruelty and irresistible power.

Two further matters are noteworthy. First, the dragon gives his power, his throne, and his authority to the beast. As the beasts in Daniel represented empires, so John's beast also represents political power. This suggests that the beast is in reality the dragon in an earthly political form. It assumes the form of a state, an imperial power. It has, however, an element that Daniel's beast-empires did not have. It has a religious aspect. Like the dragon, it receives worship from men. When empire is united with divine qualities, the union of the two results in a politico-religious structure. With it there emerges state religion, state worship, and at its centre stands the state idol. This is precisely the kind of state that the Roman empire with its god-emperor represented at the time of John. As is made very clear in Revelation 17:9,10, the beast is the city built on seven hills, the city called 'Babylon the great' (14:8), the imperial capital, Rome. It is 'the great city which has dominion over the kings of the earth' (17:18), to which authority has been given over 'every tribe and people and tongue and nation' (13:7).

The second matter worthy of particular attention is the 'mortal wound' that was healed in one of the seven heads of the beast. This wound is referred to again in verses 12 and 14. There, however, the wound is not localized in one of the heads of the beast but it simply belongs to the beast in its entirety. What this 'wound' wants to tell us, apparently, is that it is not possible to kill the beast. A mortal wound is a wound that kills. But the beast, though he has a mortal wound, is not killed. Only the Lamb when He comes in His power can kill the beast (19:20). The seven heads of the beast indicate the fulness of power in which it manifests itself. When one empire receives a mortal wound, that is, is defeated and disappears, that is not the end of the beast. It simply continues on in a succeeding empire or kingdom or other political power structure. The wound which killed one empire heals, and the beast continues in power in another empire.

In 17:10 the ten horns of the beast are identified as 'ten kings' who will receive power for one hour. This will be discussed in its place.

The character of the beast is anti-God and anti-Christian. He blasphemes God and he blasphemes the people of God. He has power to make war on the saints and to conquer them, and he has authority over all the peoples of the world. Yet none of the might which he wields is his own. His blasphemous mouth is 'given' to him, he is 'allowed' (Greek: given) to exercise authority, he is 'allowed' to make war against the people of God and to conquer them, and finally the worldwide character of his power is also 'given' to him. Even the time of his power is determined—he can exercise his authority for only forty-two months, that is, the time between Jesus' first and second coming. Meanwhile, he is widely worshipped. All whose names have not been written in the Lamb's book of life (i.e. all who have not been sealed) give him divine honours.

For John the Roman empire was the form in which the beast appeared. Doubtless, he expected Christ to return soon and establish His kingdom, perhaps even in John's lifetime. This did not in fact happen. For us, therefore, the Roman empire becomes a symbol of all human political-religious-economic power which rejects the authority of God and of His Christ and rejects and persecutes believers. The worst form in which such power can come to expression is the union of Church and state.

John concludes his description of the beast by indicating the certainty of Christian suffering while the beast has power: 'If anyone is to be taken captive, to captivity he goes.' On the other hand, he indicates the certainty that all who slay with the sword shall certainly be slain in their turn. Therefore believers are called to endurance and faith while the purposes of God are being worked out in the history of man.

5 The beast that arises out of the earth, 13:11-18

The second beast that John sees arises out of the earth. With that, the universal character of the evil trio that oppose God, His Christ, and the Church is made clear. The dragon descends from the heights of heaven, the first beast ascends from the depths of the sea, and the second beast comes up from the heart of the earth. What role does the second beast play in this great drama?

The proper work of the second beast is to persuade, instruct, and deceive men. It is therefore called the false prophet (16:13, 19:20, 20:10). It represents all those powers in society which can, and at times do, enter into the service of the godless state. Such powers today are education, science, the news media, religion, the economy, recreation, medicine, and other influential sectors of the national life.

These aspects of the second beast are indicated by John's description of it. The false prophet has two horns like a lamb. It therefore looks like an ordinary lamb and is gentle in appearance. It speaks, however, with all the blasphemy and arrogance of the dragon. Through its knowledge and understanding, it is able to perform fear-inspiring signs. It leads its followers to make an image of the first beast which is so constructed that it appears to breathe and to speak. The heart of all the works of the false prophet is lies and deception. His function is to serve the interests of the first beast, that is, the godless state whose mortal wound was healed. By that, John means to indicate that after the collapse of the previous empire, Rome now stands strong and established as the undisputed master of the world. Its agent to keep men in subjection to it is the false prophet. He works notably through the priests of the temples and altars on which sacrifice is made to the spirit of the emperor.

When a conflict develops between the two beasts and their followers, on the one hand, and the servants of God, on the other, then the false prophet forces his followers to receive a mark of recognition. It is a mark given on the right hand or on the forehead (13:16). This mark is needed for economic and social survival. In Rome the mark of the beast during persecution was the possession of a certificate that sacrifice had been made to the emperor. In the more complex societies that have developed since then, far more complete control of the population has become possible. With all the means of communication and identification available to a modern state, few are able to escape observation. All receive a number. If a state becomes anti-Christian, no believer can escape its power. John does not mention the name of the second beast, but he does mention its number. It is the number of a man, and it is six hundred and sixty-six.

In the main, scholars give two explanations of this mysterious number. One is that it represents the emperor

Nero. Profoundly hated by the Roman political leadership, he was sentenced to death by the Senate in A.D. 68. He escaped execution by committing suicide. The common people, among whom he had a large following, believed that he would one day return from the dead. This belief John is supposed to have used by making Nero the symbol of the beast that persecuted the Church and would return to do so again. In Hebrew his name was pronounced Kaisar Neron. The consonants in these two names, KSR NRON including O which may function as a consonant in Hebrew, have the following numerical value in Hebrew usage: K = 100; S = 60; R = 200 ($\times$ 2) = 400; N = 50 ($\times$ 2) = 100; O = 6: total 666.

The second explanation would appear to be more in keeping with the apocalyptic style of writing, which uses the form of symbol rather than the form of secret code. The number six falls one short of the complete or perfect number 7. A three-fold seven could well represent the fulness of God. A three-fold six would then represent the fulness or the highest power of man, falling short by one digit of the divine perfection. Many scholars therefore see the number six hundred and sixty-six as the number of the Anti-Christ. John's description of the false prophet and Paul's description of the man of sin in 2 Thessalonians 2:1-12 correspond remarkably. In both instances we should think of an organisation of society united against God which may find its highest expression in some great but evil individual.

6 The Lamb and the one hundred and forty-four thousand, 14:1-5

In Revelation 12 and 13 we met the five great opponents in the struggle between light and darkness. They are the Church and the Lord Jesus Christ, on the one hand, and Satan, the beast, and the false prophet, on the other. Each side has one outstanding champion. They are Christ and Satan.

We have observed the dragon and his two accomplices in all the fulness of their power. We have seen the Church flee to the wilderness and the Lord Jesus taken up to heaven to escape death at the hands of the dragon. That, however, is only half of the story. We now see Christ in the power of His heavenly majesty accompanied by a vast multitude of the redeemed. They stand on Mount Zion, a symbol of the heavenly Jerusalem, the dwelling place of God. The multitude with Christ is the one hundred forty-four thousand who were sealed in chapter 7. They are the first-fruits of the great harvest of the whole universe which will inhabit the new heaven and the new earth. There the Lamb will lead them and they will follow Him wherever He goes.

7   Three angels and a voice from heaven, 14:6-13

Three angels flying in mid-heaven now appear to make proclamations. The first angel proclaims the eternal gospel to all who dwell on earth. He calls on all men to worship Him who made the heavens and the earth, for the time of God's judgment has come. But, as we have noted again and again, men do not respond to the call to believe. Therefore the second angel appears and announces the destruction of Babylon. The nations that would not hear the gospel drank the wine of Babylon's sinfulness. Now is declared that the source of that sinfulness has been destroyed. Rome was not in fact destroyed in John's time. It remained the seat of world power for more than two hundred years. But her fate was so certain that her destruction is presented as having been accomplished. The meaning of that destruction we shall note more fully in the discussion of chapters 17 and 18.

The third angel warns all who associate themselves with the power which controls the evil city that they will be destroyed as Babylon was. Their destruction will take place 'in the presence of the holy angels and in the presence of the Lamb.' It was believed in John's time that life after death continued in a place under the earth called Hades. This was divided into two parts: Paradise, the home of the blessed, and Gehenna, the place of torment. The damned, therefore, are presented as suffering in the sight of the inhabitants of Paradise, and the holy angels and the Lamb are singled out as observing them.

Since believers as well as unbelievers suffer from the judgments of God in history, there is here indeed a call for patience and endurance on the part of God's people. So great is the need for perseverance and steadfastness in the faith, that a voice from heaven praises death as desirable for those who are in Christ. 'Blessed are the dead who die in the Lord', says the voice. And he adds: 'henceforth.' Christ has gained the victory and He is celebrating it in heaven. It is not yet being celebrated on earth. In pain and suffering the victory is being worked out there. A defeated enemy, vanquished, conquered, but still strong enough to gain what appear to be victories, remains to be destroyed and wholly put away. Meanwhile, blessed are those who do not have to endure the suffering of this warfare to the End. Many of Christ's soldiers are called home before the war is over. When they do go home they do not go alone. Their suffering, their services, their witness, their self-sacrifice, the whole record of their work and labour for Christ and His cause accompany them to heaven. There they rest, and the reward of the servants of God will be in proportion to their obedience on earth.

8 The double harvest, 14:14-20

The three angels in verses 6-11 all made their proclamations within the history of mankind between the first and the second coming of Christ. The four angels in verses 14-20 are the agents of the final judgment at the end of history. That judgment is presented in the form of two harvests. The picture of the double harvest is drawn from Joel 3:13, where it is a symbol of the Day of the Lord (verses 14, 15). The description of the judgment in Revelation 14:14-20 is not wholly clear. The first of the two harvests is apparently a grain harvest, but it is not explicitly stated. The second harvest is a fruit, specifically a grape, harvest. It is not indicated whether the first harvest is a harvest of the saved, as in Matthew 9:37, Mark 4:26-29, or of the wicked, as in Matthew 13:36-42, or possibly of both, as in Galatians 6:7-9. The harvest of grapes, on the other hand, is clearly a harvest of the wicked. It is thrown into the great winepress of the wrath of God, and there flows from it a spectacular river of blood four feet deep and two hundred miles long.

The agent of the first harvest, moreover, is difficult to identify. He wears a crown, looks 'like a son of man', and is seated on a white cloud. This is language such as we find in Daniel 7:13 and Matthew 26:64. Many, therefore, identify this figure as the Lord Jesus Christ, the Son of Man. It is difficult to do this, however. He is instructed to reap by an angel, which would seem to be strange. He is not related to the judgment of the wicked, for that is entrusted to an angel (verse 17). If the first reaper is the Son of Man, then the words, 'another angel came out of the temple' (verse 14) become very difficult to understand. Those who believe that the first reaper is Christ understand the earlier angel or angels (to which 'another angel' must refer) to be the three angels mentioned in verses 6-11. But there is nothing to indicate that these angels came out of the temple. Many angels appear in Revelation whose origin is not indicated.

Several reasons suggest that the reaper seated on the cloud is an angel. His co-reaper in verse 17 is definitely an angel, and it is specifically stated that he came out of the heavenly temple. Angels have appeared as men (Genesis 18:2,16; 19:1; Mark 16:5; Luke 24:4). The expression 'another angel' in verse 15 is therefore easier to relate to the one seated on the cloud (the one 'like a son of man') than to the three angels mentioned earlier. This understanding would be supported by Jesus' words, 'the weeds are the sons of the evil one, and the enemy who sowed them is the devil, the harvest is the close of the age, the reapers are angels . . . the Son of Man will send his angels . . .' (Matthew 13:38-41).

We must take particular note of the angel who commanded the second reaper to reap. He is the angel who came out from the altar and is described as 'the angel who has power over fire.' The altar is referred to as 'the' altar. It is therefore a known, a familiar, altar. It is the altar under which are the souls of those who have been slain for the Word of God (6:9). Their guardian angel commands the reaping angel to judge the world. With that, the patience to which the souls of the martyrs were called in 6:11 is fulfilled. It is with reference to such already familiar subjects as the hundred and forty-four thousand, the throne, the living creatures, and the elders that John by simple but eloquent touches unites the earlier and later parts of the book.

Finally, the wine of the wrath of God was pressed 'outside the city'. This is a clear reference to the manner of sacrificing the sin-offering in Leviticus 4:11,12, and the sacrifice made on the Day of Atonement in Leviticus 16:21-28. This symbolism is transferred to our Lord in

Hebrews 13:11-12. Sin and the sin-bearer were destroyed outside the camp, outside the holy city. Thus also in this picture of universal judgment, the wrath of God against the sin of man is revealed outside the heavenly Jerusalem (Revelation 21:27; 22:3,15). The imagery of the winepress is drawn from Isaiah 63:3, but its exaggeration is derived from the first book of Enoch 100:3: 'And the horse shall walk to the breast in the blood of sinners, and the chariot shall be submerged to its height.' The picture is one of total and unsparing judgment on evil.

Meaning for today
It is not a new thing to be told that Satan has power. Nor is it a new thing to be told that his power is limited. But when we read that

> The serpent poured water like a river out of his mouth after the woman, to sweep her away with the flood. But the earth came to the help of the woman, and the earth opened its mouth and swallowed the river which the dragon had poured from his mouth (12:15,16)

then we see scriptural teaching in the form of realities that inspire us with courage and with comfort.

For the person who observes the times in which he lives, two things cause constant amazement. One is the continuing presence of evil in the world. Education, science, even the gospel, have not removed it. If he observes closely, moreover, he will discover that evil is not found in its strongest and most influential forms among thieves and murderers and persons of bad repute. The most powerful expression of evil is in high places, in influential places, in wealthy places, in cultured places, yes, even in holy places. The second thing that amazes is the continuing presence of the good. In contrast with the forces of evil, the good is not found in the first place among the wealthy, the highly placed, the influential, the cultured. The forces of good are mainly found among the humble, the commonplace, the ordinary people. At the same time, they are by no means absent from the higher circles of life.

There is something about the good, weak though it is, that the forces of evil fear. Therefore they are always seeking to destroy it. It is because of this that Satan, the greatest of evil powers, seeks with all his might to destroy the woman. The woman that he seeks to destroy is the powerful, majestic figure who stands on the moon and is clothed with the sun. He is not, however, able to destroy her in her power and her majesty. He waits for her time of weakness when she has become a fugitive and has fled to the wilderness. It is in pursuing her there that he pours out water like a river to drown her. But the earth comes to her help. It opens its mouth and swallows the river that the dragon sends out after the woman to destroy her.

In our fear of evil, we often forget that evil is not united in its aims. The earth of which the dragon is prince and ruler often opens its mouth to defeat his plans. For this reason those who struggle for righteousness always have an ally of whom they are seldom aware. That ally is the ally of conflicting interests in the camp of evil. The good has no control over this ally. It cannot count on him. It cannot enter into an alliance with him. The good can only count on its own forces, its own weapons, its own resources. But too often these are quite inadequate. How then can the good still be victorious?

It is a part of the sealed scroll which Christ has opened that the earth swallows the waters which are intended to drown the cause of right. The people of Mozambique, Angola, and Guinea-Bissau counted on a long and grim struggle for independence from Portugal. Then, suddenly, the Portuguese front collapsed. Why? No doubt because from its side the struggle seemed as hopeless as did America's involvement in Vietnam. But the decision to give it up and follow a wholly opposite policy was not predictable. It arose from within the Portuguese community because that community was itself divided.

Again and again self-interest leads men to give up an evil course of action not because it is evil, but because it is seen to be dangerous or unprofitable or useless. The opening of the sealed scroll has something to say to us here. Somehow, Christ is present in the circumstances that lead men to abandon evil plans. The ten kings of chapter 17 will unite with the beast to destroy the harlot. Later on, these same ten kings will doubtless fight with each other. Only Christ knows what is in the seals. His knowledge of what is to be, and His control of it, is complete. Our knowledge is limited. Our strength is weak. Such as our knowledge and strength are, they can only serve in terms of hope, obedience, and trust. Where these do not bring us to victory we must exercise the endurance and faith of the saints (13:10) until Christ's own victory appears.

On the side of righteousness there are resources of which the threatened Church is unaware. In the camp of the oppressor there are self-destructive forces at work of which the Church is also unaware. The battle and the victory are Christ's. The Church must live by faith. When the dragon is about to snatch its life away, the Church cannot cause the ground to open and swallow him. This is in the hands of Him who opens the scroll. Sometimes, often, the ground does not open to swallow the enemy. Often evil is victorious. The two witnesses are killed and lie dead in the streets of the evil city. But what lies in the view of all is only their dead bodies. Their souls were sealed and protected, and the dead will rise again to the amazement and fear of their enemies. The Accuser has been cast out of heaven and the atoning death of Christ has removed every barrier between the believer and his Lord. In Christ the victory is ours. We await God's full revelation of it.

THE SEVEN BOWLS OF GOD'S WRATH

Chapters 15, 16, 19

In chapters 12 to 14 John showed us the deep mysteries lying behind the struggle between the Church and her persecutors. From this point to the end of the book all the participants in that struggle are led to their final destiny. The judgments that flow out of the last trumpet (chapters 15,16), the destruction of the great Babylon (chapters 17, 18), the victorious appearance of Christ at the head of heaven's armies and the destruction of the beast and the false prophet (chapter 19), the reward of the martyrs (20:1-10), are all presented in turn. Step by step, evil and its agents are eliminated. Step by step, the conquests of Christ and His followers are revealed. At the end there is the total separation of good and evil in the final judgment (20:11-15), and the beauty of the new heaven and the new earth overwhelm us (chapters 21,22). Thus do John's apocalyptic visions move on steadily to their great climax.

It remains then to examine the last eight chapters of the book. We begin with the final series of judgments described in the seven bowls of the wrath of God. The sixth bowl announces the impending great battle of Armageddon. The description of the battle is spread over three chapters—16:12-15; 17:14; and half of chapter 19. These must be treated together and therefore the chapter sequence which we have followed thus far must be broken. We have chosen to discuss the battle in this section in view of the massive preparation for it found in 16:12-16. It should be remembered, however, that in the sequence of symbolic events related by John, the two beasts and their armies are destroyed (chapter 19) after the destruction of the harlot (chapters 17,18). The impossibility of imposing a chronological sequence on Revelation comes strongly to the fore here.

In discussing 11:15-19 (Section VIII) we noted that the blowing of the seventh trumpet was announced but that its contents were not revealed. Many interpreters of Revelation believe that the blowing of the seventh trumpet in Revelation 11:15-19 brings the judgment of the seven trumpets to an end. They understand the lightning, noises, thunder, earthquake, and hail in 11:19 to constitute the woe that would be announced by the seventh trumpet for those who dwell on the earth (8:13). It is true that the seventh trumpet is not again mentioned by name. It is also true, as we have seen, that there is an interval of three chapters between the blowing of the trumpet in 11:15 and the disclosure of its contents in chapters 15 and 16. These circumstances may seem to support the view that 11:15-19 concludes the description of the seven trumpets. What John has to say about the seventh trumpet, however, does not allow of such an understanding. Let us take note somewhat more fully than we did earlier (Section VII) of the reasons for this.

a. In 8:13, after the first four trumpets have been blown, an eagle flying in mid-heaven cries out, 'Woe, woe, woe, to those who dwell on the earth, at the blasts of the other trumpets which the three angels are about to blow!' Thereupon chapter 9 describes the terrible contents of the fifth and sixth trumpets. The seventh trumpet, however, is not described or mentioned. Like the seventh seal, it stands apart from the others and is blown after the preparation for the last series of judgments (10:1-11:14).

b. In 10:7 an angel announces that 'in the days of the trumpet call to be sounded by the seventh angel, the mystery of God, as he announced to his servants the prophets, should be fulfilled.' This fulfillment begins to take place in 15:1, where we are introduced to 'seven angels with seven plagues, which are the last, for with them the wrath of God is ended.' The judgment is concluded in 16:17, 'The seventh angel poured his bowl into the air and a great voice came out of the temple, from the throne, saying, "It is done!" '

c. In 16:18,21 the same signs of divine power are repeated that we have met earlier in 4:5, 8:5, and 11:19. The flashes of lightning, loud noises (or voices), peals of thunder, and a great earthquake are, as before, accompaniments of divine revelation. They are not judgments but symbols of majesty and might, the earthquake fusing with the judgment of the hailstones.

d. If the seven bowls of wrath are a fulfillment of the seventh trumpet, we understand what is meant by 'with them the wrath of God is ended' (15:1) and by 'It is done!' (16:17). But if they stand by themselves alone, to what 'wrath' does 15:1 and to what 'It' does 16:17 refer?

e. Finally, as we would expect, no new series of judgments issues out of the seventh bowl. The seventh seal introduced the seven trumpets, the seventh trumpet introduced the seven bowls of wrath, but the seventh bowl gives no birth to further judgments. Its only message is, 'It is done!', for with them the wrath of God expressed in seals, trumpets, and bowls of wrath is ended.

1 The song of victory, 15:1-4

When no one in heaven or on the earth was able to open the scroll sealed with seven seals, John wept (5:3-4). When the seventh seal was opened which introduced the seven trumpets (8:1), the event was so significant that there was silence in heaven for a half hour. Now the third cycle of judgment begins to execute the seven plagues 'which are the last' (15:1). This time there is neither weeping nor silence but great joy and a mighty song of victory. Final victory is near and it is viewed as already achieved (verses 2-4).

When John sees seven angels appear with plagues, his attention is immediately turned to a scene of great power and majesty. Standing around the sea of glass which extended before the throne of God (4:6), and which is here mingled with fire, is a vast throng of people. They are those whose faith, perseverance, and self-sacrifice have conquered the beast. They have harps of God in their hands, and while they strum them, they sing the song of Moses and the Lamb. The song that they sing is only symbolically related to that sung by Moses and the children of Israel (Exodus 15). The point of connection is the conquest of Pharaoh and his army (Egypt), on the one hand, and the conquest of the beast and his image (Rome), on the other hand. Therefore it is also called the song of the Lamb. As Moses was the leader of Israel in the old dispensation, so Christ is the leader of the new. Both the old and the new song ascribe victory to God alone. It is like the worship which the elders gave to God in 11:16, when the seventh angel blew his trumpet to introduce these seven last plagues.

2   The open temple, 15:5-8

John's vision now returns to the seven angels with the seven plagues. They come out of the temple which had been opened to reveal the ark of the covenant in 11:19. That vision, which introduced the seventh trumpet, now continues. God's temple, His heavenly dwelling place and the home of the ark symbolizing God's faithfulness, stands open. Seven angels bearing seven plagues come out of it. Their dress of pure linen and girdles of gold point to the purity of their heavenly character and to the authority of their judging power. The bowls of wrath that are given to them touch the physical lives of men. They are, therefore, given by one of the four living creatures who represent the powers of God in nature (cf. Section III under 4:6-11). The bowls are filled with the wrath of the eternal and ever living God. They remind us of the words of Hebrews: 'It is a fearful thing to fall into the hands of the living God' (10:31), 'for our God is a consuming fire' (12:29). The smoke that fills the temple both reveals and hides the glory, the awe, and the mystery that surround God (Exodus 19:16-18; 40:34-38; 1 Kings 8:11; Isaiah 6:4). Only when the seven plagues had been poured out was it possible again to enter the temple. God's judgments remain a mystery until they have been executed.

3   The seven bowls of the wrath of God, 16:1-21

It may seem that there is little here that is new. The plagues poured out by the seven angels seem to be remarkably similar to the plagues inflicted in trumpet judgments in the second cycle. Along with this we note strong backgrounds in the plagues inflicted on the Egyptians at the time of the exodus. Sores afflicted men; seas and rivers turned to blood. The power of the sun was both intensified to create unbearable heat and diminished to create darkness. The drying up of the Euphrates was like the drying up of the Red Sea or the Jordan River. All of these are familiar phenomena. Moreover, in all of these, as in both the Egyptian and the trumpet judgments, men do not repent but rather turn the more strongly against God.

We must not, however, allow these similarities to obscure the very important differences that the bowls of wrath present. We shall list the more important of these.

a. The most significant difference between these last plagues and the preceding judgments is that they are not partial in their effect, but total. There is no question here of a third of the earth being burnt up or a third of the sea becoming blood or the end of suffering after five months. As the judgments contained in the trumpets were more severe than the judgments contained in the seals, so the bowls of wrath are more severe than the trumpets. The bowls of wrath provide the final opportunity for repentance.

b. The seventh angel closes the account of the plagues by pouring out his bowl into the air. The previous six angels all poured their bowls on some object: the earth, the sea, the rivers and fountains of water, the sun, the throne of the beast, and the river Euphrates. The seventh bowl does not have a particular reference. It is simply poured into the air. The opening of the scroll in 6:1 began the cycle of the seven seals. The seventh seal began the cycle of the seven trumpets. The seventh trumpet began the cycle of the seven bowls. The seventh bowl is not the mother of the new cycle. It marks the end of all the cycles. With its being poured out, a voice from heaven cries, 'It is done!'

c. The scroll which the Lamb opened has now revealed all its contents. They revealed both God's patience with and judgment on the sinful human race. Again, as at earlier crucial points in God's dealings with men, there are flashes of lightning, loud noises, peals of thunder, and an earthquake to symbolize the divine power. This time, however, the earthquake destroys 'the cities of the nations' in particular. There is a plague of mighty hailstones so that men curse God. These developments presumably are closely associated with the battle of Armageddon, possibly suggesting the manner in which

107

the victory of the Rider on the white horse (chapter 19) was achieved. This battle we must now consider more closely.

4   The battle of Armageddon, 16:12-16; 17:13,14; 19:11-21

When the bowl of the sixth angel is poured out, it dries up the waters of the Euphrates River. The way is now open for the kings of the east to approach. John has used the symbol of the Euphrates before. In 9:14 it was the boundary that separated the Roman empire from the world around it. Here, in 16:12, with his usual freedom he makes it a boundary between the forces of evil and the Christian homeland. The drying up of the great river removes all restraint upon the kings of the earth and their armies to attack the people of God.

The dragon, the beast, and the false prophet co-ordinate their planning of the assault. Out of their mouths come evil spirits like frogs whose ungainly form, slimy bodies, and huge, bulging eyes are a fit symbol for the repulsive spirits of the demonic world. The spirit sent forth by the dragon is an emissary from hell, which is the home of the dragon; the spirit sent by the beast operates in the political and economic world; the spirit from the false prophet represents false religion. Together they go out to deceive the kings (leaders) of the world in every area of life, to assemble the forces that will oppose Christ and His followers. The site they have chosen for the battle is a place called Armageddon.

In John's vision Armageddon has a purely symbolic value. The name comes from two Hebrew words: *har*, meaning mountain, and *Megiddo*, the name of a city in north-central Israel overlooking the valley and plain variously called Jezreel, Esdraelon, or the Plain of Megiddo. Here two militarily significant highways crossed each other. One ran from Egypt north to Syria and Mesopotamia; the other led from eastern and central Palestine to the Mediterranean coast. Great battles had been fought on the Plain of Megiddo. John therefore makes Armageddon (or Mount Megiddo) a symbol of the final meeting between the forces of good and of evil pictured in 19:19: 'And I saw the beast and the kings of the earth gathered to make war against him who sits upon the horse and against his army.' When and where and how the actual spiritual confrontation which Armageddon points to will take place is not disclosed. What is revealed is that unseen powers of good and evil, moving behind the visible earthly scene, will marshal their forces for the final test of strength between the Lamb and the dragon.

We are not left in uncertainty, however, as to the outcome of the battle. As the forces of darkness prepare for the conflict, so do the forces of light. Their preparation does not consist in a fearful council of war to plan strategy for a battle of dubious result. The preparation is a celebration of victory that is regarded as already achieved. God has judged the harlot! The smoke of her goes up for ever and ever! The marriage of the Lamb has come and His Bride has made herself ready. The Lamb who was mighty to open the scroll sealed with seven seals has all power in heaven and on earth. Therefore every creature sings, 'To him who sits upon the throne and to the Lamb be blessing and honour and glory and might for ever and ever.' And the four living creatures and the elders shout 'Amen!' (19:1-10).

When John has seen this display of celestial power and joys, he sees heaven opened and in it he sees a white horse standing. A Rider sits on it who is Faithful and True and in righteousness he makes war. His appearance reminds one of John's first vision of the glorified Christ. His eyes are like a flame of fire. Many crowns adorn his head. He has a name that no one knows but himself. His robe is dipped in blood and he is called the Word of God. Heaven's armies dressed in white follow him. With a sharp sword that comes out of his mouth he will strike the nations and govern them with an iron rod. On his robe and on his side a name is written: 'King of kings and Lord of lords.' He it is who will be the instrument of God's fury against the enemies of the truth.

Two aspects of this description deserve attention. First of all, we are struck by the emphasis given to the names of the Rider on the white horse. He is called Faithful and True. He has the name the Word of God. He further bears the name King of kings and Lord of lords. He has still another name which no one knows but himself. The significant thing here is not simply the titles of Christ, meaningful though they are. It is rather the fact that these are His *names,* that He is *called* by such and such a *name.*

In the Bible the names applied to God and to His Son are not merely names and titles, as we normally understand these, that is, designations of identity or dignity. Their significance is that they *reveal* who and what God and His Son *are*. Their names are, in a sense, identical with them. 'The name of the Lord is a strong tower; the righteous man runs into it and is safe' (Proverbs 18:10). It is in this significance of 'name' that the reason lies for the commandment, 'Thou shalt not take the name of the Lord thy God in vain.' In a similar way must we understand that Jesus at His exaltation received a name that is above every name (Philippians 2:9). So here, the names ascribed to Christ describe to us His deepest being, His deepest self. There is, however, one name that is given but not disclosed. It is the name that only Christ Himself knows. His having such a name indicates His oneness with his brethren who also have such a name (Revelation 2:17). Comment is made on this in Section III, Part 4f and need not here be repeated.

The second point to observe is that He will rule the nations with a rod of iron (19:15). Any consideration of Christ's rule over the nations must begin with the authority that was given Him at His resurrection. He said, 'All authority in heaven and on earth has been given to me' (Matthew 28:19). It is *this* authority, not a new or an additional authority, that governs the nations with a rod of iron. It is the same authority as that which makes possible the Christian witness in the world, 'Go *therefore* and make disciples of all nations' (Matthew 28:18). The basic character of this authority is that it enforces and maintains the law of God the Creator, which redemption enables the believer to keep, however imperfectly. The heart of the law is: 'You shall love the Lord your God with all your heart, and with all your soul, and with all your mind . . . and . . . you shall love your neighbour as yourself' (Matthew 22:37-39).

The failure to live by this law brings its own consequences. Christ's upholding of this law in the life of the nations means that He maintains a law which they, as a whole, reject. This rejection separates them, to the extent that they reject it, from God, the source of life and joy and peace. The iron rod of Christ consists in the self-created hatreds, economic exploitation, working at cross-purposes, wars, social unrest, crime, corruption, personal hostilities and alienations of all sorts—in short, the pains and the sorrows of mankind. To them, as well as to Paul in the days before his conversion, apply the words: 'It is hard for you to kick against the pricks' (Acts 26:14). As we noted in discussing the judgments of the seven trumpets, the judgments of God are indeed judgments of God, but they come by way of self-induced penalties for the rejection of His law.

It is noteworthy that in Revelation 2:26,27 believers are given the same power over the nations that Jesus has. 'I will give him power over the nations, and he shall rule them with a rod of iron . . . even as I myself have received power from my Father.' This power would appear to be the prayers of the saints for their deliverance from persecution. We noted the influence of prayer on the life of the nations in our discussion in Section VII, Parts 2, 3, and 6. The power of the saints and the power of Christ to rule the nations with a rod of iron doubtless meet in the intercessory work of Christ, as expressed in Romans 8:34, 8:26-27 (Christ and his Spirit are not to be separated) and Hebrews 7:25. It is especially noteworthy that in Romans 8:34-37 Christ's intercession is directly related to both the suffering and the conquering of the saints.

Christ's ruling the nations with a rod of iron, mentioned in connection with the battle of Armageddon, raises the question of the time duration of that battle. The immediately following *Meaning for Today* makes some observations about this.

Concerning the battle itself nothing is said. Only results are indicated. The forces of the beast apparently never have a chance to put their carefully planned assault into action. The beast and the false prophet are captured and destroyed. All the distinguished leaders whom they had inspired, their knowledge, their might, their imposing and frightening organization are laid low in a moment, like an encampment of tents before a tornado. Of all this power men had said, 'Who is like the beast, and who can fight against it?' (13:4). In one stroke, consuming all human might, pride, and greatness, the kings of the earth and their armies become carcasses, food for the vultures of heaven. All this is done by the Rider on the white horse. The armies of heaven, also mounted on white horses, had followed him to Armageddon. It is not recorded that they participated in the battle.

Concerning the means of victory, one thing should be noted. The enemy was slain 'by the sword of him who sits upon the horse, the sword that issues from his mouth' (19:21). This 'sword' is his tongue and therefore points to a warfare of words, ideas, and beliefs. The great and ongoing struggle in which all believers are taken up is not against flesh and blood, but against the principalities, against the powers, against the world rulers of this present darkness, against the spiritual hosts of wickedness in the heavenly places (Ephesians 6:12).

Meaning for today

It is significant that the battle of Armageddon is reported at the end of the third and last cycle of judgments. When the last bowl has been poured out, a voice from the heavenly temple cries, 'It is done!' The seventh bowl brings us to the end of human history. What is the meaning of Armageddon for men living in the twentieth century?

The universality of the last cycle of judgments corresponds to the worldwide unity of mankind that shall at that time have come into being. John saw 'the beast and the kings of the earth with their armies,' gathered to do battle with the Rider on the white horse (19:19). Armageddon witnessed the assembled might of 'the kings of the whole world' (16:14). We of the twentieth century are able to view this in a way that was not possible in earlier times. In the course of the present century more has been done to make communication on a world scale possible than in all preceding centuries together. This is a direct result of the technological revolution. The steamship, the train, the car, the telephone, telegraph, radio, TV, the telex, the computer, the press have revolutionalized communication in ideas and in travel. Out of this have arisen the world organization of the United Nations, continental or regional associations of nations in Africa, the Americas, Europe, and Asia. It makes possible the mammoth international corporation, far-reaching academic and cultural exchange, global economic and financial structures. It has also made possible two world wars and the threat of nuclear war.

It is against this background that readers of Revelation

today must understand the meaning of Armageddon. The demonic spirits of the dragon, the beast, and the false prophet assemble the organized power of mankind for battle on the great day of God the Almighty (16:14). Against this array of power the Rider on the white horse goes forth at the head of the armies of heaven (19:11-21). The conflict is therefore universal in extent and final in time.

There has in the meantime come into being another universality that we may not fail to note. It is the universality of the Church arising out of the worldwide preaching of the gospel. The Church is today not only universal in its essential character and in its intention, but it is actually spread over the entire world. Neither its weaknesses, failures, or defeats, nor the opposition to it of anti-Christian forces have been able to prevent this worldwide expansion. When the combined might of mankind shall be united and the Church shall have declared its testimony to all men, then and not until then shall the End come. Its early coming has often been proclaimed, but never has it been possible to say it with so much support in the form of international structures and communication.

Even so, we must be very careful how we say these things. What amazes us today will be the familiar and normal thing of tomorrow. The work of the first computers that occupied the space of a large room is now done more efficiently by a portable device on your desk. We have no more conception of what the world of 2100 will be like than the people of 1850 were able to foresee either the complexity or the potential for good and evil of our contemporary society. But more, God's thoughts are not our thoughts. In all prediction of the way in which Christian hope will unfold, we do well to remember the admonition of our Lord: 'It is not for you to know times or seasons which the Father has fixed by his own authority' (Acts 1:7).

In any case, before the End can come, Armageddon must take place. What does this mean?

By Armageddon we understand a final confrontation between the forces of darkness and the forces of light, between those who are Christ's and those who are not. While having all kinds of physical aspects, the confrontation is basically spiritual in character. It arises out of the fact that darkness cannot tolerate light. Even the merest flicker of light is a threat to the domination of darkness. For this reason the power of the gospel is out of all proportion to the numbers or the social importance of those who believe it. Where it is preached, however weakened its condition, it is a threat to the godless, beast-inspired power structure. It must therefore be eliminated.

The basis of all suppression of believers will be the absence in them of the mark of the beast. Their life and testimony will make it clear that they do not 'belong' to the society that is controlled by the beast. Social and economic discrimination, family pressures, exclusion from the normal pursuits of education and livelihood will all be used to make men worship the beast. When this fails, the naked power of the state will be applied. Penalties and imprisonment and the shedding of blood may follow, and the Church will become an even smaller society. The dead bodies of the witnesses will be exposed to public gaze, and this will lead to great rejoicing. When the Son of Man comes, will he find faith on the earth?

When we speak of the 'battle' of Armageddon we are inclined to think of an event of very limited duration. The battles about which we read in the history of warfare were usually only hours in duration and seldom longer than a few days. As soon as a battle becomes a conflict of ideas, however, its time extent lengthens immeasurably. The 'battle for men's minds' is often fought to the third and fourth generation.

The description of Armageddon leaves the impression of a lightning-like, momentary encounter. The enemy is suddenly and totally destroyed and no losses are suffered by the winning side. When we read this we may not forget that we are dealing with apocalyptic imagery. The completeness of the victory is pictured in the language of total destruction. It will be recalled, however, that in discussing the judgments of the seven trumpets we took note of their character. We observed that God's judgments often arise out of the operation of His own created laws in men, in society and in nature, as also from the interaction of these upon each other. To what extent such factors will be active in the final test of strength between Christ and Satan and their followers we cannot know. But it would not be wise to leave these possibilities out of consideration.

At all events, we do know that the conflict will coincide with a high expression of the unity of mankind. The unity will not be one simply of relatedness through the communication of ideas and travel. Beyond that we see a world government, a world economy with a levelling out of the differences between developed and developing countries, and some form of shared world culture.

In the confusing and rapidly moving history of our time there are several factors that bear on these considerations. One is the vitality and hidden power of the developing countries. Who can tell what great part they are to play in continuing history of mankind? A second is the decadence that is in many ways characteristic of the present wealthier countries. There is also the role that nuclear power may play, hopefully beneficially but very possibly destructively, and on a scale that is incalculable. The day may not be far distant when the smaller countries and even urban guerrillas under sophisticated leadership will be able to manufacture atomic bombs. Lastly, there is the role reserved for the gospel and the Church in this shortening time of the End. In the West the gospel sun may be setting. In Africa it is approaching high noon. In the vast Far East it has in some countries hardly or not yet risen, while in others it seems to hover permanently at dawn level.

Massive are the mighty forces, challenging and frightening are the opportunities that lie in the womb of the future. How grateful we should be that all power over these things is in the hands of the Lord Jesus Christ, to whom has been given all authority in heaven and on earth.

How far off, how near, is the consummation that we have been contemplating? Who would dare say? But equally, who among those who discern the movements of history would dare to question that in our very time Armageddon is very much in the making?

THE HARLOT AND THE BEAST

Chapters 17 and 18

The climax of Revelation does not come all at once. It comes in stages spread over six chapters and these culminate in the glorious vision of the new Jerusalem coming down from heaven like a bride to meet her husband. First we see the defeat of the forces of evil. The harlot is completely destroyed (chapters 17 and 18). The Rider on the white horse captures the two beasts and casts them into the lake that burns with brimstone (chapter 19). Last, Satan is captured and is thrown into the same fiery pool (20:11-15). While these mighty events are going on, the martyrs receive a reward for their suffering and faithfulness (20:1-10). Then indeed comes the End with the final judgment (20:11-15), and the revelation of the new Jerusalem (chapters 21 and 22).

Such are the contents of the last six chapters of Revelation. In this section we consider the character and the judgment of the harlot and the victory of Christ over the two beasts.

1 The harlot and the beast, chapter 17

From the viewpoint of apocalyptic symbolism and imagery, chapter 17 is one of the most difficult in the book. Specifically, the problem is to see the interrelationships between the harlot and the beast with its seven heads and ten horns. It will help to separate and list the main elements that pertain to each. Then we shall be in a better position to relate them to each other in an ordered whole.

a. The harlot

1. She is seated on many waters (verse 1). These waters represent peoples and multitudes and nations and tongues (verse 15).

2. The whole earth commits fornication with her (verse 2).
3. She is seated on a scarlet beast and is clothed with abominations (verses 3-5).
4. She is drunk with the blood of saints and martyrs (verse 6).
5. She is seated on seven hills which are the seven heads of the beast (verse 9).
6. The beast and its ten horns will destroy the harlot (verse 16).
7. She is the great city which has dominion over the kings of the earth (verse 18). She is also called 'Babylon, the mother of harlots' (verse 6).

b. The beast
1. It carries the harlot and has seven heads and ten horns, and it is full of blasphemous names (verses 3,7).
2. The seven heads of the beast are seven hills; they are also seven kings; five of them have fallen, one is now reigning, and one is still to come (verse 10).
3. The beast that was and is not will ascend from the bottomless pit and go to perdition (verse 8). It is also said to be an eighth but it belongs to the seven (verse 11).
4. The ten horns are ten kings. They are still to appear and will receive authority with the beast for a short time (verse 12).
5. The ten kings will give their power to the beast and together they will make war on the Lamb, but the Lamb will conquer them (verses 13,14).
6. The kings and the beast will hate the harlot and destroy her (verses 16,17).

When we analyze these data in the light of chapters 12, 13, and 14, we can come reasonably close to an understanding of what John meant to say through them. The harlot is clearly the city of Rome, which was at the height of its power in John's day. She is seated on the famed seven hills on which Rome was built. The 'many waters' are the peoples, tribes, and nations that were governed by Rome (cf. Section IX, Part 4). The scarlet beast that carries her is the political, economic, religious power of the two beasts that we met in chapter 13. In order to share in her wealth and pleasure the leaders and people of the Roman world are willing to sell their honour and their integrity.

The advantages which they gain from their service of Rome are in fact abominations and impurities. They involve, then as now, injustice, social and economic discrimination, struggle between 'haves' and 'have-nots', bribery, moral degeneration, the use of law and the courts to cover up corruption, the protection of crime, religious persecution. Yet in the very society in which this disintegration was taking place, the arts, literature, architecture, jurisprudence, and economic power were advancing. Since such a society cannot tolerate witness to the truth, there is much suppression of just protest in her. Therefore the harlot becomes drunk with the blood of the martyrs.

The beast on which the harlot sits is more difficult to describe. On the one hand, it is perfectly clear that the beast is identical with the harlot. The harlot is Rome; the seven heads of the beast are the seven hills of Rome, i.e. Rome itself. On the other hand, it is equally clear that the beast represents far more than the city of Rome. The heads of the beast also represent seven kings, five of whom have fallen, one of whom now reigns, and one of whom is still to come. Its ten horns are ten kings who are to receive power for awhile. These will unite with the beast to destroy the harlot. In addition to these there is the highly mysterious statement that the beast that was and is not is an eighth and belongs to the seven (verse 11). How must we understand the identity of beast and harlot and, conversely, their separateness and distinctiveness?

When we consider the beast and harlot in the light of all that Revelation says about them, we see two fundamental ideas in John's presentation. The first is that the beast is the Satan-inspired earthly power which in all the comings and goings of human history *is always in the world*. The beast constantly changes the *form* in which it manifests itself, but it never changes *itself*. The beast in his historical manifestation assumes now this appearance, then that, but its basic character as the Satan-inspired earthly power remains always the same. Its own character is *a constant factor* in history.

The second basic idea in John is that the harlot is a specific temporary historical form in which the beast expressed itself. This form was the political, economic, military, and religious society and state known as the Roman empire, of which the city of Rome was the governing centre. Relating these two thoughts in a unified whole, we may say that the harlot is a *temporary* manifestation of the beast as a *constant* reality. It is for this reason that the beast and the harlot are, on the one hand, identical; on the other, distinct. In the harlot we meet the beast in the same way in which in a regiment we meet the army. A regiment may be disbanded or totally destroyed in battle, yet the army remains.

This understanding probably explains why in chapters 12-14 the harlot does not appear alongside the dragon and the two beasts, other than in the one reference to her as 'Babylon' in 14:8. The harlot *is* both of them so long as they wish to express themselves in such a form. The fact that John devotes two chapters almost entirely to the discussion of the harlot shows the great importance of this form in the strategy of Satan and the beasts. Nevertheless, when their strategy responds to the ongoing changes in history, and the harlot no longer serves their purposes, she is destroyed. This would appear to be the meaning of the destruction of the harlot by the beast and the ten kings in 17:6.

It may also be noted that the second beast (13:11-18), namely the false prophet of 16:13, 19:20, and 20:10, is not mentioned in either of the chapters 17 and 18. It is included in 'the beast' and is therefore included in the harlot as an expression of the beast. For this reason the harlot is 'drunk with the blood of the saints and the blood of the martyrs of Jesus' (17:6), who are the special object of the hatred of the false prophet.

2 The seven heads and ten horns of the beast, chapter 17

The relationship between the beast and its seven heads and ten horns is more difficult to understand than the relationship between the beast and the harlot. We meet again the problem of identification and difference, but there is less data to relate them into a satisfactory whole. We shall first discuss the relationship between the beast and its seven heads.

The first time we meet the 'seven heads' in Revelation is in the initial description of the dragon in 12:3. 'And another portent appeared in heaven; behold, a great red dragon, with seven heads and ten horns, and seven diadems upon his heads.' In 13:1 we are introduced to the beast 'rising out of the sea, with ten horns and seven heads, with ten diadems (crowns) upon its horns and a blasphemous name upon its heads.' In these two verses the dragon and the beast receive almost identical descriptions. The dragon has seven heads and ten horns. The beast has ten horns and seven heads. In the case of the dragon the seven heads have crowns; in the case of the beast the ten horns have crowns, and a blasphemous name is written on its heads.

In 17:3 the beast on which the woman sits is 'full of blasphemous names and it had seven heads and ten horns' (mentioned in the same order as in the case of the dragon, 12:3). In 17:7 the beast is again described as having seven heads and ten horns. In 17:9 the heads are said to be the seven hills on which the woman is seated, and in verse 10 they are described as seven kings, five of whom have fallen, one is, and the other has yet to come. When he does come, he will remain only a little while.

We have already considered the relationship of the seven heads to the seven hills on which the harlot sits. Our interest now is to understand how the seven kings can be seen as five that have fallen, one that is now reigning, and one that is still to come, and then only for a little while.

Some commentators consider that the seven kings refer to individual Roman emperors of whom five had died, one was then reigning, and one was still to come. But this view has great difficulties. Assuming that John wrote in the reign of Domitian (A.D. 81-96), there had been eleven emperors up to his time. In order to reduce this number to five who had fallen and one who was still alive some very strange historical judgments have to be made. Moreover, five of the seven had 'fallen'. This is a strange word to use about dead emperors, particularly since Augustus, Tiberius, Vespasian, and Titus had died normal deaths while in possession of the emperor's office. And which of the remaining emperors who reigned in the Western Roman empire up to 476 is the 'one' who was still to come?

In view of these considerations it is more acceptable to view the seven heads of the beast as empires rather than as emperors. The close relationship between king and kingdom in the ancient world makes kingdom or empire a valid understanding of 'king' in verse 10. One can point to five great empires that preceded the Roman. They are the Old Babylonian, the Assyrian, the New Babylonian, the Medo-Persian, and the Greco-Macedonian empires. The sixth would be the Roman empire, and the seventh was still to come. The difficulty of this interpretation is that according to it there was but one empire to arise after the Roman. This would mean that from 476 on, or at the latest from 1453 up to today, we have been waiting for the 'one' and final empire to appear.

The view that therefore commends itself most is that not only do the 'kings' refer to empires, but also the numbers seven, five, and one must be understood symbolically. This is especially true of the number seven. It is used scores of times in Revelation and always in a symbolic context. The number seven would then in the present instance not refer to seven distinct empires but to the full number of world powers that would appear up to the time of Christ's return. Five is a broken and incomplete number (in distinction from the frequently and symbolically used three, four, seven, ten, twelve, thousand) and suggests that of all empires that have been and shall be, the greater part has come and gone. One existed in John's time and 'one' was still to come. This last 'one' does not mean a unit of one, that is to say, a particular, a certain empire, but rather it suggests smallness, brevity, shortness. The larger part of history is past. The Church had at Christ's resurrection entered upon the 'three and one-half years'. Only a short segment remains for the kingdom of man on earth. John was standing in the End-time and expressed himself accordingly.

It would appear that the ten horns of the beast must be seen in close association with its seventh head. The ten horns and the last head have several remarkable things in common. One is that the seventh 'king' and the ten 'kings' represented by the horns will be contemporary with each other. This is specifically indicated by the fact that the seventh king, when he comes, 'must remain only a little while' (verse 10), and the ten kings will receive authority as kings 'for one hour' (verse 12), which is another way of saying a little while. Moreover, they will have this authority 'together with the beast', and they 'will give over their power and authority to the beast' (verses 12, 13). In short, they will act in concert.

We must be careful in our reading about the beast and its heads and horns not to divorce them from each other as though they were separate and distinct beings or powers. The seven heads and the ten horns are the heads and horns *of the beast*. It is through them that the beast acts and speaks and exercises its authority. They are *different aspects* of the *one being* that is called the beast. The character of these aspects would seem to be obvious. The figure 'head' represents the instrument of leadership: vision, hearing, speaking, and especially intelligence and thought. The figure 'horn' represents the instrument of execution. In the Bible the horn is the symbol of power, might. In other words, the world powers carry out what the beast plans and commands. They are the beast in its various manifestations in history. We must return to this in the part *Meaning for Today*.

3   The beast that was and is not and is to come, 17:7-13

It is said of the beast (i) that it was and is not and is to ascend from the bottomless pit and go to perdition (verse 8a); (ii) that it was and is not and is to come (verse 8c); that it was and is not and is an eighth but belongs to the seven, and it goes to perdition (verse 11). We have seen that the seven heads are inseparably a part of the beast. It is always through one of the seven heads that the beast acts and expresses itself. Of these heads five have come and gone, *one is*, and one is still to come. This led us to conclude that although the heads may change, the beast who acts through them *is always in being*. The beast is a *constant factor* in human history. Now we read no less than three times that it 'is not'. This means that at the very time when the sixth head 'is', the beast that has that head 'is not'. Further, when the beast at last appears, he will ascend out of the bottomless pit (verse 8; cf. also 11:7) and then go to perdition (verses 8, 11). There is only one place in Revelation where a similar situation is found. It is in 20:1-10, which speaks of the binding of Satan, his being confined in the bottomless pit, and his release from it. This is the more worthy of note because according to 13:1, in connection with 12:3, Satan appears to be identical with the beast. Before he was bound in the bottomless pit

Satan *was.* During the one thousand years that he is bound, he *is not,* so far as mankind is concerned. When he is released he comes up out of the bottomless pit and after a short time goes to perdition. When that happens, however, the harlot, the beast, and the false prophet have all been destroyed. It is therefore difficult to establish a relationship between the beast that was and is not and is to come in chapter 17 and the binding and the release of Satan in 20:1-10.

This uncertainty also makes it difficult to speak with any assurance about the eighth head of the beast which 'belongs to the seven'. A suggestion can, however, be considered. The seventh manifestation of the beast may culminate in such an increase in the exercise of its demonic power that it could be considered to have become an eighth head. Its difference from preceding manifestations of the beast would therefore be one of degree, not of kind or basic character. Therefore it would properly 'belong to the seven'. The constant description of the beast as having seven heads makes it reasonable to associate the 'eighth' head with the seven in some such manner as here suggested. The New Testament lends support to such a supposition. Jesus said that the tribulation in the final days of this world's life will be so severe that if they were not shortened no human being would be saved, and if possible even the elect would be led astray (Mark 13: 20-22). Similar strong indications of inexpressible danger for the Church are given in 2 Thessalonians 2:3-12, Revelation 20:7-10, and notably Revelation 11:7-10.

4 The destruction of the harlot, 17:15-18:34

The harlot is destroyed by the beast in alliance with its ten horns, i.e. ten kings. Its destruction is a marked example of the need to distinguish between the beast as a constant factor in human history and the harlot as a temporary manifestation of this constant factor. It cannot be said that the beast destroys itself. It can, however, definitely be said that the beast destroys particular manifestations of itself. As the institutions, forces, and movements of society change, the strategy of Satan changes with them. A method of operation that was useful in one period of history becomes ineffective in a later period. It must therefore be disposed of and new modes of operation be devised. We need to remind ourselves of the strictly symbolic language of Revelation. When studied carefully, the symbolism makes sense. Indeed, it makes powerful sense. Only occasionally after the long remove of nearly two thousand years are we unable to follow John's meaning.

In the beast-harlot-heads-horns complex we are dealing basically with one individual personality, namely the beast. At any given time in history the beast as harlot, the beast as head, and the beast as horns will exist simultaneously. The beast as beast can be seen only in these historical manifestations. Further, we must remember that history and symbol fade into each other. Consequently, it is usually difficult to judge where history ends and symbol begins. Sometimes history itself is a symbol, as we shall see below.

The difficulty in separating history and symbol certainly comes to strong expression in the destruction of the harlot. John intended the harlot to represent Rome. There can be no question about that. But what must we understand by its 'destruction'? Rome was never destroyed. As a city it has a continuous history up to the very present, and this history now counts more than two thousand five hundred years. Much of the Rome of John's time fell into decay as the result of gradual depopulation and neglect. But even today buildings and monuments are standing in Rome that were there when John wrote Revelation. Present-day Rome is a modern city built on the site of and around the ancient city. It can, of course, be said that the city represents the empire. Even so, it is the *city* that represents it and John is talking about the city.

It can therefore not be said that Rome went up in smoke. Neither fire from heaven nor from the torch of man ever set it aflame. The burning of Rome in A.D. 64 affected only a district of the city where the poorest of the poor lived. Some believe that Nero himself gave it over to the flames and then blamed the Christians for it. The destruction of Rome is therefore a doom that can overtake any economic-political-cultural-religious complex at any time in human history. The burning, the fire, and the smoke give to such a destruction the colouring of an event of the End-time when, according to frequent biblical teaching, the world will be consumed in a universal conflagration. John's burning of Rome therefore indicates not so much a ruin by fire as an eschatological event, that is, an event of the End-time, pointing to the final judgment of all evil in the world.

It is in this light that we must review the 'ten kings' which function as servants of the beast. It is they who with the beast destroyed Rome as the centre of a great world power. How was this Rome 'destroyed'? How did it decline from its wealth, magnificence, power, and population of more than a million people to a poor and unimportant town of 20,000 in the Middle Ages? This came about through forces and movements in history, whether economic, social, political, migratory, religious, or otherwise. Important among these were the removal of the capital of the empire from Rome to Constantinople in the fourth century, the invasion of the tribes from east of the Rhine, north of the Danube, and from Africa, and the end of the Roman empire in the West in 476. Such forces and movements are, on the one hand, under God's control and part of the history which He is guiding to its destiny. On the other hand, the forces of evil are deeply embedded in the structures of human society and they know how to use developments in them. The judgment of the harlot is therefore a process in which both demonic and divine forces are involved. This is clear from John's description of the judgment:

> And the ten horns that you saw, they and the beast will hate the harlot; they will make her desolate and naked, and devour her flesh and burn her up with fire. (17:16)

The very next verse, however, adds:

> For God has put it into their hearts to carry out his purpose by being of one mind and giving over their royal power to the beast, until the words of God shall be fulfilled.

Even clearer is 19:2 and its context in showing that the destruction of the harlot is a judgment of God:

> Hallelujah! Salvation and glory and power belong to our God, for his judgments are true and just; he has judged the great harlot who corrupted the earth with her fornication, and he has avenged on her the blood of his servants.

It would be difficult in all the Bible to find a more telling example of the truth of Paul's words: 'For we cannot do anything against the truth, but only for the truth' (2 Corinthians 13:8). It will be useful in the context of the present discussion to refer to Section VII, Part 3 where some observations are made on the nature of God's judgments.

When, therefore, Rome, the historical Rome, city of emperors and popes, is regarded as a symbol, John's use of it becomes of permanent value. Revelation is a book of the Church for all time and for all peoples. What it says about Rome it says about any economic-political-religious complex that is inhabited and governed by men who make self and their desires rather than God and His service the centre of their lives.

The destruction of the harlot invites reflection on the nature of her wealth and power as revealed in chapter 18. This we shall do in the discussion below.

Meaning for today

There is probably no greater contrast in the international world today than that between the 'developed' and the 'developing' nations. Few stop to consider the precise meaning of this contrast. Does it mean that the 'developed' nations enjoy a beneficial ripeness in all respects and that the 'developing' nations are following far behind them? Does it mean that Africa and Asia are less developed than the West in their family relationships? In Europe and in America it is usual for seventy-year-olds to live and die in commercially maintained homes for the elderly because there is no room or desire for them in the homes of their children. Is this a part of the West's superior development? Are the two world wars of this century, which had their origin solely in the West, a symbol of this desirable development?

When one takes a close look at the notions of 'developed' and 'developing' (or, as some put it, 'under-developed') countries, he soon discovers that what is meant is largely an *economic* distinction. A more direct way of describing the developed-developing distinction is the 'haves' versus 'have-nots' contrast. And the 'having' and the 'not-having' relate to money, resources, and manufacturing in the world of business and to the comforts and amenities of life in the world of the home. They also relate, and in no small degree, to education, health, communications, and technology. But here again, on close inspection, we discover that all of these sustain a truly close relationship to the wealth of the 'haves' and the poverty of the 'have-nots'.

It is, therefore, of interest to note how largely the harlot is described in economic terms. She is definitely a 'have'. And the merchants who do business with her are 'haves' because of her. A substantial part of chapter 18 is devoted to setting this forth. Verse 3 says that 'the merchants of the earth have grown rich with the wealth of her wantonness'. The chapter is pervaded by a deep sorrow because now 'no one buys their cargo anymore' (verse 11). This cargo is varied indeed. Verses 11-13 list no less than 29 articles of trade, and these are doubtless but a small part of the commodities that were sold and traded. They range from fine linen and scented wood to cattle and horses and the souls of men. Such was the merchandise with which Rome's shops and storage places and markets were filled.

This trade and commerce were carried by ships. Rome was a sea power. Ships, shipmasters, and sailors brought to Rome's harbour the products of countries that her armies had conquered. For the ships that came to Rome with cargo there were in the homeland scores of large and small businesses and thousands of traders, office employees, artists, labourers, farmers, and slaves. On their backs the merchants stood who grew rich by Rome's wealth. The 'merchants' who served Rome and who were served in turn by the thousands who produced their merchandise were not merely businessmen. They were leaders from every part of society, 'the great men of the earth' (verse 23). The harlot controlled the *whole* of the lives of the men who grew rich from serving the harlot. All had the mark of the beast. All worshipped it. To be successful depended on being a genuine part of the society that made the harlot the harlot. To be accepted in Rome meant to be honoured in one's home city or in one's homeland, whether that was Syria or Spain or Egypt or Greece. The mark of the beast was the willingness to do whatever Rome required to be successful. Did success require a straightforward, honest business deal? Then be straightforward and honest. Did it mean paying a bribe to get a contract or make a sale? Then pay the bribe. Did it mean spending an adulterous evening to please the circle in which you did business or had your recreation? Then so spend the evening. The god you worship is success. If he demands your best, give him your best. If he demands your worst, give him your worst. Right and wrong, good and evil, are irrelevant considerations. Success, becoming more a 'have', less a 'have-not'—that is what counts.

The effort to become a 'have' without regard to right or wrong can create strange situations. Throughout the West the ever increasing depletion of natural resources to meet consumer demands is causing problems of major proportions. In the human area, great poverty in the larger cities can exist alongside of great wealth. The striving to become a 'have' too often sacrifices considerations of justice and compassion to economic concerns. On the other hand, in a welfare state like Sweden there are no poor people. Everyone is a 'have'. But it is becoming clearer and clearer that being cared for by the government from birth to death is not developing but is rather undermining the national character.

In developing countries we find equally strange developments. It is not unusual for fortunes to be made by a politically and economically powerful elite while the poor become poorer. Brazil is fast moving from a 'developing' to a 'developed' country in terms of national wealth. From 1968 to 1974 it had a high annual growth rate of 10 per cent. But only five per cent of the people were better off because of this and the other 95 per cent were as poor in 1974 as they were in 1968. Nigeria, made rich with oil money, gave large salary increases to all government employees in 1975, forcing private companies to increase their wage scales. The resulting inflation so pushed up prices that the masses of the people who were employed neither by government nor by the 'private sector' could buy less for their money than before.

These inequalities, whether between nations or within nations, have religious significance. The economic aspect of the harlot should not hide the fact that she was first and foremost a religious power. The harlot is an incarnation of the beast. The beast is the earthly representative of Satan. Satan is against God, against Christ, against God's good creation, and therefore against the Church which bears the new humanity. Satan, the beast, and the harlot are all representative of a creature-God relationship which is the opposite of that which God made and intended. They represent a creature-God relationship which is not expressed in love and light but in hatred and darkness. That is why the beast is full of blasphemous names. That is why the harlot is drunk with the blood of saints and martyrs. In the context of this discussion, how is economic power related to the true, the deepest, character of the harlot?

There is no area in life in which love for self, the priority of a person over his neighbour, the priority of a person over God, comes to such clear expression as in the relationship of a person to material possessions, especially money. Its power lies in its convertibility. It is changeable into whatever is purchasable. Things purchasable are not only shoes, cars, houses, meat, and bread. Honour, purity, high office, influence, confidences are also purchasable. A great statesman once said, 'Everyone has his price.' This is, of course, not wholly true. The two witnesses, the martyrs, did not have their price. They had been purchased by the blood of Christ. Therefore they did not worship or carry the mark of the beast. But the statement is often very largely true. The enmity of the beast and the harlot is against those who will not sell themselves. Their warfare is the continuance in a million different forms of the first temptation: 'you will be like God. . . . So when the woman saw that the tree was good for food, and that it was a delight to the eyes, and that the tree was to be desired to make one wise, she took of its fruit and ate, and she also gave some to her husband, and he ate' (Genesis 3:5,6).

When a man's deepest desire is for something other than doing the will of God, his pursuit of that desire is false worship. The proper name for it is idolatry. The proclamation by the beast and his prophet that the values they represent are the highest good is their blasphemy. And the practice of these values as the highest good is the wine of abomination in the golden cup of the harlot that makes men drunk.

An unhealthy religiosity may lead men to believe that to be a 'have' is sinful and to be a 'have-not' is a blessing. The absurdity of such thinking becomes plain when it is applied to possessions less measurable than material things. Is it a sin to have knowledge and a blessing to be ignorant? Is it a sin to enjoy health and a blessing to be weak and ailing?

The Christian solution is both more difficult and more promising. The 'haves'—be they nations, corporations, or individuals—should examine how they became and remain the 'haves' that they are. And the 'have-nots' should ask themselves whether in the pursuit of a larger share of this world's good things they will end up becoming all that they now criticize in the 'haves'. Both will find their answer in the demand to love our neighbour as ourselves, and God above all. Such love must find *economic* expression in terms of Amos's 'Let justice roll down like waters, and righteousness like an overflowing stream.'

THE REWARD OF THE MARTYRS AND THE FINAL JUDGMENT
Chapter 20

Our study of Revelation has brought us to its most difficult and also its most controversial subject. It is the question of the millennium. Nowhere else in the Bible is any reference to be found to a thousand-year kingdom to be governed by Christ and resurrected saints. This is found only in the twentieth chapter of Revelation, but there the reference is clear and explicit. This chapter is inseparably connected with chapters 17, 18, and 19, and all these together with chapters 12 to 16. We must now see how chapter 20 stands related to the foregoing chapters and to the book as a whole.

1 The thousand years, 20:1-10

a. Major data relating to the millennium
1. The binding of Satan

In chapters 18 and 19 we witnessed the destruction of the harlot and the two beasts. The time for Satan's judgment has now come. Unlike the others, his destruction is not immediate. He is first imprisoned for a thousand years and then, after a brief return to power, he is totally destroyed. During his imprisonment he is bound with a chain and is kept in a bottomless pit which is locked and sealed over him. It does not appear that he can have any communication with the world that he once governed through the harlot and the two beasts.

2. The reign of Christ and the martyrs

The description of the thousand-year reign begins with a vision in which John sees thrones on which are seated 'those to whom judgment was committed'. That those who sit on the thrones are the risen martyrs is a reasonable inference. But it is an inference; it is not specifically indicated. Of the martyrs it is specifically said that 'they reign with Christ a thousand years'. Whether this reign includes the judgment just referred to, we cannot positively say. It is also not clear whether the reign of the saints takes place on earth or from heaven. Presumably it is on the earth, for the martyrs are raised from the dead. Nor are we able to say who are judged, over whom Christ and the martyrs reign, or what happens on the earth during the time of their reign. The millennium is pictured with a beginning and with an end, but not a word is spoken about its nature, its content, the course of its history, or its purpose. Theological imagination has filled this period with all manner of activity, but it has done so without scriptural support. Only Revelation 20 speaks about the millennium and therefore what is not said about it there, is not said about it anywhere.

3.   The rest of the dead

That the martyrs are raised from the dead is clear. There is, however, a difference of opinion among translators whether the words at the end of verse 4, 'and who had not worshipped the beast or its image', refer to the martyrs or to believers who were not killed for the sake of the gospel. The grammatically approved translation is, 'I saw the souls of those who had been beheaded . . . namely those who had not worshipped the beast or its image.' On this reading 'the rest of the dead' who did not come to life again until the thousand years were ended includes all who have died, whether believers or unbelievers, except the martyrs. These will all be raised in the second resurrection described in verses 12 and 13.

4.   The release of Satan

Why the release of Satan 'must' take place (verse 3) is not explained. Verse 7 suddenly and, as we have noted, without any account of millennial history having been given, transports us to the end of the thousand years. At that point we see a remarkable thing. Powerless believers are gathered together in a 'camp', presumably near Jerusalem 'the beloved city', surrounded by mighty armies of enemies that have been gathered by Satan. Many questions arise at this point. Where do the armies of Gog and Magog come from? Were the 'ends of the earth' in fact under the millennial reign? In the absence of the harlot and the beast and the false prophet, what means did Satan use to deceive the nations? Revelation gives no answer to these and similar questions. It simply states that fire came down from heaven and consumed the enemies of the saints, and that Satan was thrown into the lake of fire into which the beast and the false prophet had already been cast.

5. The armies of Gog and Magog

The reference to Gog and Magog places the background of 20:7-9 squarely in chapters 38 and 39 of Ezekiel. The prophet there received a command: 'set your face toward Gog, of the land of Magog, and prophesy against him' (38:2). God's wrath will be aroused and Gog with all his vast armies that have been gathered from the north and from the south will be destroyed. In Ezekiel, then, Gog is a king and Magog is a nation. In Revelation Magog remains a nation and Gog is also regarded as a nation. Outside of the references in Ezekiel, the Old Testament does not know a nation by name of Magog nor a king by name of Gog. Their use in Revelation is, therefore, even more mysterious. What is very clear, however, is that they represent the forces of the Anti-Christ in the End-time.

In summary, the millennium of Revelation is described in terms that are in many ways unclear and therefore invite many questions. It invites expectations of a long and happy period of a thousand years between our present troubled history and the introduction of the eternal state. During that time all the fearsome evils occasioned by the harlot, the two beasts, and Satan will be wholly absent from the earth. Risen martyrs under the leadership of the risen Christ will reign. Evil will be able to arise only out of the sinful heart of man. But this evil will not be tempted or provoked by the four hellish powers, which will be either dead or in prison during the millennium. The holy examples of the risen martyrs and the risen Lord will stimulate men to love and good works. Such a society will be without even the faintest precedent in the history of mankind.

Over against this most appealing picture stands the fact that the rest of the Bible, even the rest of Revelation, has nothing to say about such a final period of human history. John gives no indication what role the millennium will play either in history or in God's plan of redemption. Moreover, Revelation 20:1-10, with all its uncertainty, stands in a book that is more symbolical in character than any other book in the Bible. It should, therefore, not surprise us that the history of interpretation of the millennium is a very mixed history and also a very inconclusive one. It is to this that we now turn.

b. Four major historical interpretations

By 'historical interpretation' we mean a view of the millennium which regards it as a period of historical time in which, in one way or another, the rule of Christ and the martyrs does or will take place in human affairs before the final judgment and the resulting eternal state occurs.

1. Premillennialism

The name is derived from the belief that Christ's first return will take place before (from the Latin *pre*) the millennium is established. There are many schools of thought among premillennial believers, but they hold the following teaching in common. There will be two returns of Christ and two resurrections. At His first return He will destroy the satanic power, raise up all the dead in Christ, and gather together all living believers. Among these will be many Jews who have turned to Him and acknowledged Him as the Messiah. He will govern the world in righteousness for a thousand years or, as many have it, for a rounded but extended period of time. This will be a period of great spiritual and material progress. At its end Satan will be released from his prison and will seek to destroy the believing community. Christ will then come from heaven a second time and destroy Satan and all his works. The second resurrection, that of all who were not included in the first, will then take place, the final judgment will be held, and the eternal state will begin.

2. Amillennialism

The name indicates the belief that there is no (from the Latin *a*) millennium. It is not a wholly correct description of the view that the amillennialists hold. They reject completely the idea of a special spiritually and materially fruitful period at the end of human history, in the sense in which premillennialists believe this. They do, however, definitely believe in a millennial reign of Christ and the saints. In their view the thousand years of Revelation 20 began with the first coming of Christ and will extend to His second and final return. During this period Satan is bound only in the sense that he can deceive the nations no longer. The gospel can therefore be preached everywhere and the Church established. At His first coming, Jesus 'bound the strong man', i.e. Satan (Matthew 12:29), and now through the preaching of the gospel is plundering his goods. The entire period from the first to the second coming of Christ is, therefore, the millennium. Of it the thousand years are a symbol. This view was first expressed by the North African theologian Tychonius (about 390) and was popularized and given status in the Church by Augustine. Both the Roman Catholic and the traditional Protestant churches hold to his view.

3. Postmillennialism

This view teaches that Jesus will return after (from the Latin *post*) the millennium to judge the world and introduce the eternal state. Through the preaching of the gospel and the work of the Holy Spirit the millennium will, as it were, come into being of itself. This interpretation was popular at the end of the last and the beginning of the present century. But two world wars, constant political and social turmoil, and the emergence of Africa and Asia as powerful segments in the world community have completely discredited this basically Europe-centred view of history.

4. Dispensationalism

This teaching is basically premillennial. It has, however, a view of the plan of redemption that sets it off from other premillennial teachings. Central in its teaching is the role that is said to await the Jewish people. God's dealings with men are divided into seven dispensations. A dispensation here may be defined as a given period of time in which God's relationship to men is governed by a certain principle or rule. The seven dispensations are: Innocence (Adam); Conscience (Cain to Babel); Human Government (Babel to Abraham); Promise (Abraham to Moses); Law (Moses to Christ); Grace (the entire period of the Church from the first coming of Christ to His second coming); Kingdom (the millennial period from the second coming of Christ till the final judgment).

The central concern of dispensationalism is with the last period, that of the kingdom. The millennial kingdom arises out of the fact that when Jesus offered the kingdom to the Jews, they rejected His offer and crucified Him. Nevertheless, all the promises of God given to Israel in the

Old Testament will be fulfilled. They are not fulfilled in the Church. The Church is the fruit of the work of Jesus which Jewish rejection unexpectedly made available to the Gentiles. It is, therefore, called a 'mystery parenthesis'— Grace—between the dispensations of Law and Kingdom. The promises of the Old Testament made to the Jewish people, therefore, await fulfillment. This will take place when the Church will have been taken to heaven in the rapture and the Jews brought back to the Holy Land. There they will accept Christ, who then will establish His millennial kingdom. The temple will be rebuilt and sacrifices will again be offered as in the old covenant. At the end of the millennium Satan, who had been bound and banished at its beginning, will be released for a short time and will then be destroyed. Then will follow the resurrection and the judgment. Thereafter, the Church will be eternally in heaven and the Jews on the earth.

The basic difficulty of all these views is that they consider a symbolic way of speaking to be a description of actual history, whether future or present. Dispensationalism carries this so far that the Church becomes a divinely blessed accident and will in eternity be for ever separated from its Jewish fellow-believers in Christ. Amillennialism asks us to believe that we are now, and for more than nineteen hundred years have been, living in the millennium. The premillennialists, rather than reading Revelation in the light of the Bible as whole, take their point of departure from Revelation 20 and read the rest of the Bible in its light.

If therefore, none of the historical interpretations is acceptable, what view must we take of Revelation 20, especially its verses 1-10?

c. The reward of the martyrs (a symbolical interpretation)

The common element in the views reported above is that figuratively or literally all make the thousand years the centre of their concern. In one way or another there must be a millennium. In one way or another a whole dimension must be added to history for which Scripture as a whole gives no support. This should be sufficient reason to look elsewhere for the central message of these verses. The key to finding this message would seem to be the martyrs. Consider again the emphasis of the book. It is a book about the suffering Church. Indeed, Revelation does not know a Church that is at peace. It knows only the Church under the cross of persecution. As a result of its persecution of the Church the world suffers the judgments of God. But in the widespread agony reported and represented in Revelation the suffering of the children of God is central. It is in a sense the continued suffering of the Lamb that was slain.

The suffering of the Church is symbolized especially by the suffering of the martyrs. They are tortured, they are beheaded, they are killed. Their dead bodies are allowed to lie in the streets of the city. In heaven they cry to God for justice and vengeance. The martyr is the hero figure of Revelation. Chapter 20 is the last chapter that deals with the history of the Church on earth. Before John brings his account of history to an end, he sets forth the martyrs finally as victors in the struggle. He singles them out for special distinction. He depicts them as reigning with Christ on the earth for a thousand years. Harlot, beast, and false prophet are dead. Satan has been conquered, bound, and put out of the way. And they, the martyrs, are raised to life in the body along with their victorious Lord, and they reign in a world in which the powers that so long afflicted them are totally vanquished and undone.

That is the picture that John draws. And let us make very plain that it is a *picture*, not a happening in history, not a future event. For a moment he draws the martyrs out of the shadows of the cross into the bright light of victory, peace, and joy. He gives them royal honours along with the great martyr who is now Lord of lords and King of kings. They have suffered with Him, now they are glorified with Him. Weeping may endure for a night but joy comes in the morning. That is the picture that John draws.

There is no binding of Satan, there is no millennium, there are no resurrected martyrs while believers who suffered less are left in their graves. There are no hosts of Gog and Magog who threaten to bring their time of victory and rejoicing to an end. This is all apocalyptic framework and background to say this one thing: 'Well done, you good and faithful servants. You have been faithful in a little, I will make you rulers over much.' Physical suffering for Christ's sake is not the only standard whereby God measures excellence in His kingdom. The beatitudes in Matthew 5 mention this as but one among other virtues that God will highly reward. In Revelation, however, the martyr is the supreme symbol of loyalty to Christ, of endurance, meekness, faithfulness, obedience, and love. This symbol, the martyr, John honours by picturing him as reigning in victory and peace for one thousand years.

When we interpret Revelation 20:1-10 as the reward of the martyrs rather than as a millennium, we do not thereby solve all problems of interpretation. With respect to the return of Christ we are at the present time very much in a position similar to that in which the Old Testament believers were with respect to His first coming. They knew *that* the Messiah would come. They did not know when, where, or under what circumstances He would come. The fulfillment of the prophecy was needed to understand the prophecy fully. It may well be so now. Those who love and look forward to the appearance of the Coming One are unable to agree among themselves about the character of that appearance. It would, therefore, seem wise to acknowledge the possibility that a view other than our own may in the end prove to be the correct one. Meanwhile, we must live by the understanding to which we come through a conscientious study of the Scriptures.

There is one general principle of scriptural interpretation which I believe to be worthy of special consideration at this time. It is the principle that Scripture is its own best interpreter. When this principle is taken seriously, it would seem reasonable to believe that Revelation 20 should be read in the light of the Bible as a whole rather than the Bible as a whole in the light of Revelation 20.

2   The final judgment, 20:11-15

John concludes his visions of the trials of the Church and of God's judgments on the world as he had begun them in chapter 4. He sees a throne and Him who sat upon it (20:11, as in 4:2). So glorious and overwhelming is the majesty of the last vision that earth and sky flee away from it and disappear. Before the throne he sees all the dead gathered, great and small, to await the divine verdict on their lives. An act of the profoundest significance underlies the rendering of this verdict. The books were opened and 'the dead were judged by what was written in the books, by what they had done'. What are these 'books'?

The idea of books being used in the final judgment has considerable background in apocalyptic literature. John freely drew his imagery from this source. In one of his visions Daniel wrote, 'As I looked, thrones were placed and one that was ancient of days took his seat . . . the court sat in judgment and the books were opened' (Daniel 7:9,10). 2 Baruch 24:1 says, 'The books shall be opened in which are written the sins of all who have sinned, and again also the treasuries in which the righteousness of all who have been righteous in creation is gathered.'

While we cannot conceive of actual books being written to record our lives, there is a sense in which the term 'books' carries a very deep and significant meaning. It is the ability to remember, to recall, to live and hear and see again in our memory the past that we have lived. This ability is far, far greater than we generally think it to be. Studies in psychology show that in actual fact we forget nothing of what we have consciously experienced. Under adequate stimulus the mind is able to recall all conscious experience in the whole of its lifetime.

The evidence seems to indicate that everything which has been in our conscious awareness is recorded in detail and stored in the brain and is capable of being played back in the present. The feelings which were associated with past experiences also are recorded and *inextricably locked* into those experiences. These recorded experiences and feelings associated with them are available for replay today in as vivid a form as when they happened. . . . These experiences cannot only be recalled but also relived.[1]

The experiments from which the above conclusion is drawn also establish, however, that the memory function is not only mental or psychological, but also biological, i.e. physical. Memory functions through the physical brain. Can there be memory without a brain through which to recall? It is the consistent teaching of the Christian religion that spirit or soul can exist apart from the body. Materialistic science denies this, but a growing body of modern scientific research strongly tends to

1 Report on 'Memory Mechanisms,' A. M. A. *Archives of Neurology and Psychiatry*, 67 (1952):178-198 in *I'm O'K—You're O'K* by Thomas A. Harris. M.D.. Avon Book, 1969, pp. 25-32.

accept this as possible.[2] This is all the more remarkable since science, in distinction from faith, deals with the verifiable, the measurable. In this view death does not destroy the record of our conscious past. Forgetting may therefore be said to be an inability to remember a record that exists and for the recall of which an adequate stimulus cannot at the moment be produced.

The opening of 'the books' in Revelation 20:12, therefore, may well be the stimulation of our recall capacity by the inconceivable events of the Day of days and the powerful impressions conveyed by them. It is this very real possibility that makes the words of Jesus more than a figure of speech: 'I tell you, on the day of judgment men will render account for every careless word they utter; for by your words you will be justified, and by your words you will be condemned' (Matthew 12:36,37).

There is another book which will also be opened on the day of judgment. It is the book of life (20:12). In this book only names are recorded. They are presumably the names of the elect, written down 'from the foundation of the world' (13:8,17:8). The election of Israel to nationhood and to service, and of the individual to salvation and to service is, according to the common testimony of Scripture, an act of God's undeserved goodness. It is not based on human worth or merit. This is perhaps the reason for the names of the elect being written down 'from the foundation of the world'. This removes the idea of any human contribution to man's election. At the same time, election is never separated from life. The dead were judged 'by what was written in the books, by what they had done' (verse 12), and again 'All [including the elect] were judged by what they had done' (verse 13). Nevertheless, 'the second death' is the fate of anyone whose name 'was not found written in the book of life' (20:15). There is, therefore, a strange but vital connection between 'the books' of our deeds and 'the book of life'. The first records man's works, the second God's work. The first records events in time, the second an event in eternity. This is a mystery we are unable to penetrate.

2 'Parapsychology: Religion's Basic Science', by J. Schoneberg Setzer, in *Religion in Life*, Winter issue, 1970, pp. 595-607.

Meaning for today

All life begins with a birth and ends in a death. Between birth and death life may be infinitely varied, but beginning and end are the same. Yet in this sameness there is a difference and the difference is great beyond measure. Vegetation, insects, birds, fishes, and animals do not have to give to the Creator an account of the life they have lived. For the most lovely flower and for the most ferocious animal, death is not only the end of life, it is also the end of existence. This is not true of the form of life that we call human. For human beings there is a judgment after death and a life beyond death.

Man has been made in the image of God. That is the reason for the difference between the life of man and all other forms of life. As the Preacher says, 'God has put eternity into man's mind' (Ecclesiastes 3:11). He has been made a steward of all that God gave him, and he must account for the manner in which he has discharged that stewardship. For this reason there is a judgment.

This judgment no one, no one at all, in the whole history of mankind, is able to escape. John writes: 'And I saw the dead, great and small, standing before the throne, and books were opened' (20:12). Terrible and beautiful are the words, 'great and small'. In this world of injustice, oppression, and naked power, these words are the refuge of the innocent weak, and they should be the terror of the unjust mighty. Many years ago the Preacher saw the facts of life as they were, and they have not changed since his time. 'I saw under the sun that in the place of justice, even there was wickedness', and again, 'I saw all the oppressions that are practised under the sun. And behold, the tears of the oppressed, and they had no one to comfort them!' (Ecclesiastes 3:16, 4:1). When we see bribery in the village, bribery in the city, bribery in the international community of commerce, diplomacy, and finance, when we see corruption, intimidation, misrepresentation, and favouritism at every level of society—then we must think of the words: 'great and small, standing before the throne, and books were opened.'

In our present life justice is by no means dead or powerless. Again and again we see 'great' men, who are often in fact great scoundrels, brought to fall. Again and again we see 'small' men, who are often in fact men of noble character, cleared of false charges and their accusers put to shame. This is public knowledge. But the condemnation of the corrupt and the clearing of the innocent seems always to come as a surprise. These get headline attention in the newspapers, especially the condemnation of the corrupt. Justice is too often an unusual thing; it is not the expected, the normal, thing like health, sunshine, and rain. And the effort to achieve even this limited justice is demanding and costly. The loopholes in the law are so many, the evidence so difficult to obtain, the possibility of delay, postponement, and bribery so great, that more evil goes unjudged than judged.

In the judgment before the great white throne none of these devices will clear the guilty or hide the innocence of the just. The 'books' that will be opened will not be faulty police records, falsified bank accounts, fearful witnesses to be examined, or conflicting evidence to be weighed. The 'books' that will be opened will be the very words and deeds of men and women as they are engraved in in-erasable letters in their own remembrance and con-sciences. No one will be able to escape from the witness of his own life and history. Indeed, before the court sits to judge, the record is plain and evident to the all-seeing eye of God. Before him 'no creature is hidden, but all are open and laid bare to the eyes of him with whom we have to do' (Hebrews 4:13).

This teaching of sacred Scripture is an encouragement and comfort for the oppressed Christian. It can, however, become a temptation for the weak-willed and fearful Christian. The final judgment of God on evil does not allow us to surrender our responsibility to stand for right and justice in our own church, family, business, social, and political relationships. All true justice among men is a forerunner and pointer to the final judgment of God. It is part of the patience of God which intends to lead men to repentance so that they may be found innocent in His judgment (Romans 2:4). Only when such effort fails may we be comforted by the knowledge that failure is not the end of the matter. The defeat of justice in the human court means the postponement, not the destruction, of justice. We must then exercise ourselves in the kind of patience commended to the saints who cry for justice from beneath the altar.

THE ETERNAL CITY

Chapters 21 and 22

The end of war and persecution, of pain and sorrow, can come with great suddenness. In the crucible of suffering it is so easy to forget that the heavenly throne-room of Revelation 5 with its majesty, might, and peace never ceases to exist. In a moment, in God's moment, its power and beauty burst forth and set the sufferer free. Then the darkening clouds pass and the sun shines again with brightness on the earth. So it was in the year 323 in the early Church when the victories of emperor Constantine released the Church from horrible persecution. The church historian Eusebius describes the occasion:

> Men had now lost all fear of their former oppressors. Day after day they kept dazzling festival; light was everywhere, and men who once dared not look up greeted each other with smiling faces and shining eyes. They danced and sang in the city and country alike, giving honour first of all to God our sovereign Lord as they had been taught. . . . Old troubles were forgotten and all irreligion passed into oblivion; good things present were enjoyed, those yet to come eagerly awaited. (*History of the Church*, Book 10, par. 9)

The joy of the early Christians was but a shadow of the great celebration that will fill heaven and earth when Christ's final victory will have been attained. Throughout Revelation the joy has been anticipated. Saints and angels have sung of the victory that in Christ is already real. But men on earth cannot see it; they can only know it, they can only believe it. Faith has not yet become sight. They are still in prison, still under threat; even in freedom they are still exposed to the power of the beast. But now the harlot is dead, the beast destroyed, Satan cast out, and the last judgment held; the peace of God fills all the land. This peace John describes in the last two chapters of his book.

1 The new heaven and the new earth, 21:1

We have called attention more than once to the fact that John did not intend to describe the whole of the Church's life. He deals with the Church from the viewpoint of suffering and persecution only. Other aspects may be alluded to, but they are not discussed or made a part of the book's plan. So it is with the description of the condition of eternal glory that the work of Christ has brought into being. The abbreviated description of it comes to expression in two ways: in the renewal of all things, that is, of creation; and in the renewal of the Church. He describes the former in one verse: 'Then I saw a new heaven and a new earth, for the first heaven and the first earth had passed away, and the sea was no more' (21:1).

The words 'heaven', 'earth', and 'sea' must be correctly understood. John lived in a time when the earth was considered to be the centre of the universe. Students of astronomy have shown how vastly different the real situation is. The earth orbits around a star called the sun. This star and the earth and other bodies attracted to the sun are collectively called the solar system. This system is a part of a vast body of stars known as the Milky Way galaxy. This galaxy or 'star city' is in turn one of millions of galaxies which together make up the universe.

Although John did not know this, he undoubtedly did know Psalm 8: 'When I look at thy heavens, the work of thy fingers, the moon and the stars which thou hast established; what is man that thou art mindful of him'. In the wonderment of the Psalmist, John's view of the universe and ours can meet. He saw it all—the earth on which he stood and the heavens above him—renewed and made serviceable to God and man. In this renewed earth the 'sea' was no more. John did not behold here an earth in which there were no seas and oceans. In apocalyptic imagery the sea is the home of the beast out of which it came. It is the nations endlessly at war with God and with one another. Such an earth 'was no more'. Instead, he saw man's natural home, the green earth and the friendly heavens, made new to serve again the purpose for which God had made them. Precisely wherein the renewal consists he does not say. We can, however, form some conception of this when we try to imagine a world in which the excesses of heat and cold, the catastrophes of drought, flood, epidemic, tornado, earthquake, and crop failure, of wars and rumours of wars, no longer exist. God will again see what He has made, and He will declare that it is good with a goodness that cannot be destroyed.

2 The new Jerusalem, 21:2-8

The remainder of John's description of the new world is confined to the Church. He concentrates on this as the centre of the new creation. The Church, we may say, will be the soul of the body of the universe. Reaching deep into Old Testament imagery, John calls the Church a city, specifically the new Jerusalem. In the old Jerusalem had stood the temple with its Holy of Holies in which was the ark, the symbol of God's presence with His people. In that Jerusalem the kings had lived, the prophets had spoken, from there enemies had led Israel captive, and in it the covenant people had crucified the Lord of glory. Now John sees the Church as a new Jerusalem, dressed in spotless white to be presented to her husband, a picture of innocence, purity, and love.

John characterizes the Church in two ways. The first is that God will be with His people. Uninterrupted fellowship with God, total union with Him—that will be the essence of life in the new city. Out of that fellowship and union all other good things flow, for God is the source of all joy and goodness and holiness.

The second is the banishment for ever from the life of man, of tears and death and mourning and crying and pain. These are the 'former things' which have no place in the life of the new humanity. They have all passed away. In the full light of noon there can be no darkness. When God is all and in all, there is no room for anything that does not agree with His truth.

These two qualities are repeated in a different way in verses 5-8. The God who is the Alpha and the Omega of history has now travelled the whole way from the Beginning to the End. He says, 'Behold, I make all things new.' His people can now drink without payment from a fountain that gives the water of everlasting life. This is the reward for having conquered in the fight against all that displeases God. Therefore God sees the work of salvation brought to completion and He says, 'It is done.'

The other quality is the absence of any defiling influence in the city. It may seem at first glance that only grossly and openly sinful people are excluded from the holy community: murderers, fornicators, sorcerers, idolaters, and all liars. But be not deceived. Jesus said that everyone who hates his brother is a murderer. Idolatry can be very refined. The liar can appear in the form of the harmless lamb of truth. The cowardly who dared not stand for the right, and the spiritually as well as the morally polluted, are excluded from the city.

3 The measurements of the city, 21:9-21

The perfection of God's dwelling among men is shown in the dimensions of the city. It lies foursquare, and its length, width, and height are the same. The measuring angel finds its size to be the length of 12,000 stadia. This is equivalent to about 1,500 miles. Whether this means that the length, width, and height are 1,500 miles together, or whether each side is 1,500 miles, makes little difference. A city that is 375 miles high is just as inconceivable as one that is 1,500 miles high. We are not reading sober measurements here but apocalyptic symbols. The symbol is not fifteen hundred miles but 12,000 stadia. The length is the same but the number is not. It is number, not length or height, that we are concerned with. Each side (or all sides combined) consist of the measurement 3 x 4 x 10 x 10 x 10. This can also be read 12 x 1000. These are all numbers which in Revelation symbolize fulness, completeness. The three is derived from such prominent natural phenomena as water, consisting of liquid, steam, or ice; measurement: length, breadth, height; family: father, mother, child. The four is derived from the directions of the compass: east, west, north, and south. Multiplied, they make the frequently used number twelve. Ten is a round number which when it is squared makes one hundred and when it is cubed makes a thousand. The new Jerusalem, therefore, is perfect in size. It is ample, spacious. The city is also beautiful to see. It is made of pure gold and of jasper, a dark green precious stone. The walls have twelve foundations and all are adorned with jewels. Each of the twelve gates of the city is made of a single pearl. Since a pearl is hardly as large as a man's fingernail, the description is overdone in typically apocalyptic fashion.

In each of the four walls there are three gates. Facing east, west, north, and south, they indicate the universality of the Church. It stands open to the whole world. Over the gates of the city are written the twelve names of the tribes of Israel. Inscribed on the twelve foundations of the walls are the twelve names of the apostles of the Lamb. Walls and foundations therefore represent the fulness of the people of God, the old and the new covenants, the prophets and the apostles, Israel and the Church.

Although the city is at least 375 miles high, its wall is only 144 cubits, that is, about 220 feet. Presumably that is its height. This should not bother us. The important thing is not that so tall a city has so low a wall. John himself writes that the city has a great, high wall' (verse 12). It consists of a height of 12×12 or $3 \times 4 \times 3 \times 4$ cubits. Anything of such a size or number in apocalyptic imagery is complete, adequate, perfect.

4 Inside the city, 21:22-22:5
John's vision now takes him inside the city. What he sees there emphasizes the believer's relationship to God and to his fellow men. It stresses what may be called the quality of life.

John 'saw no temple in the city'. In earlier visions, John had seen a temple in heaven: 7:15; 11:19; 14:15,17; 15:5-8; 16:1,17. The basic idea represented by the word 'temple' in religion is a three-fold one: a structure, in which the deity is believed to dwell or manifest himself and in which his people worship him. In Israel these three elements came together at first in the wilderness tabernacles, later in the temple in Jerusalem. The house of worship, God's presence in it, and the covenant community at worship—this is what John understood by 'temple'.

The death of Christ with its attendant rending of the veil between the Holy Place and the Holy of Holies abolished for ever the idea of a localized presence of God. The disciples continued for awhile to worship in the temple, but the days of that worship were numbered. After the destruction of the temple in A.D. 70, no Christian community undertook to rebuild it, whether in Palestine or elsewhere. Worship, however, continued, and the presence of God through the Spirit was a powerful factor in it. The worship normally took place in the houses of believers. Not until late in the second century did the often persecuted Christian minority begin to erect houses of worship or 'churches' as we would call them.

Moved by long tradition and familiarity with the temple of Jerusalem, John continued to depict the presence of God as localized, even in heaven. God dwelt 'in the temple'. There His saints worshipped Him. Out of it came angels from His presence. The smoke of God's glory filled it, and out of it issued the voice of Him who sat on the throne. Now John sees the restored creation. In his vision the new heaven and the new earth have come. He sees God's presence in them as it was in the old creation before sin marred man's relationship to God. He communed with Adam in the cool of the evening (Genesis 3:8ff). Their fellowship needed no tabernacle, temple, shrine, or cathedral. So it will be in the new Jerusalem. Had John written Revelation in a later period of Christian history, he would probably have written, 'I saw no church in the city'. The dwelling of God is with men, and He Himself will be with them. The Lord God Almighty and the Lamb are themselves the temple. Their presence makes even the lights of nature, sun and moon, superfluous. John exhausts his apocalyptic vocabulary to say what Paul says elsewhere: God will be all and in all.

In turning to the garden of Eden for his symbolism of God's presence, John introduces other features from that source. As a river flowed out of Eden (Genesis 2:10), so now a river flows from the throne of God and of the Lamb. There is also a tree of life. Indeed, there appear to be more than one, perhaps many, for it stands on either side of the river. The fruits of the tree and the waters of the river are both life-giving. They are a sort of heavenly sacrament which constantly renews the life of the redeemed.

It was not possible, however, for John to confine his symbolism to the garden of Eden. There had been a long and complex history between the beginning and end of human existence on earth. A garden, however beautiful, cannot do justice to this history in describing it. Already in

John's time the world had become to a large extent city-centred. The Creator who has laid the gifts of technical skills in the heart of man does not despise the products which those gifts have brought into being. It is especially in the city that they are found. God accepts the city as a legitimate form of life. But it is the *new* Jerusalem which He accepts to dwell in. Those who practice abomination and falsehood will have no place in it. Moreover, it will be an unusual city. The garden is united with it. The river of God with trees of life on its banks is in the heart of the city. The urban and the rural meet to make the garden-city of the redeemed humanity.

Reading this description reminds us of the vision that had been given to Paul nearly a half-century earlier:

> I know a man in Christ who fourteen years ago was caught up to the third heaven—whether in the body or out of the body I do not know. God knows . . . and he heard things that cannot be told, which man may not utter. (2 Corinthians 12:2-4)

Such descriptions may lead us to think that between this life and the life hereafter there exists only a great discontinuity, an unbridgeable gap. When life is described in terms of what man has never seen or heard, and of what cannot be uttered, we seem to confront a world totally unfamiliar, wholly unrelated to anything we know. To think thus about the life to come would be a great error. There will be continuity as well as discontinuity between the age that now is and the age that is to come. As a man who is converted to Christ becomes a new person while yet remaining definitely the same man, so the world that is to come will be the same as, though wholly different from, the present world. To the disciples' eyes, knowing only this world, the risen Christ was unrecognizable (Luke 24:31). When they were opened to see the dimension of resurrection reality, they saw the familiar features and the familiar form of their teacher and friend. We must remember that the symbols John uses deal with qualities, spiritual rather than material forms, internal relationships rather than outward shapes.

It must, therefore, not surpise us that familiar things are found in the city that John has described. Kings, we read, shall bring their glory into it; they will bring into it the honour and the glory of the nations (21:22-27). The 'glory' and the 'honour' of the nations implies far more than political power and prestige. Rather, it suggests the sum total of the nations' achievements and attainments in all areas of human endeavour. In the ancient world as well as in tribal traditions to this day the king or the chief represents the life, the peace, the prosperity, of the whole people. As the embodiment of his people, therefore, the king will bring the glory and the honour of his people's history into the new Jerusalem. How is this to be done?

Since the days when Cain built his city, and Jubal made musical instruments and Tubal-cain forged tools of bronze and iron (Genesis 4:17,20,21), man has been a cultural creature. The Latin word *colere* means to tend, to care for, to till the soil. From it come the English words cultivate, cultivation, with their basically agricultural meaning. The same word that is used for the development and care of the field to make it productive has come to be used for the development and care of the human spirit to make it spiritually productive. We speak about the *cultivation* of mind and spirit and of their gifts. The resultant product we designate as *culture*. Alongside of this dimension, though quite distinct from it, stands the English word 'cultus', referring specifically to the art of organized group worship or the ritual of worship.

The fruit of man's cultural activity comes to its highest and most developed expression in the great cities of the world. It is there that the famous universities, with their libraries, learned teachers, and laboratories, are found. There, too, are the theatres for drama, song, and music, studios for painting and sculpture, the noblest products of architecture, the exercise of political power, the means of industrial production, the display of wealth, the scale of military might. There, too, are frequently found the finest expressions of a people's character, their virtues, their distinctive gifts and qualities—reasoning and art in Greece, organization of government in Rome, religion in Israel.

But this is only one face of the city. The other face is its shame, its cruelty, its immorality. The Roman merchants traded not only in wonderful creations of culture, but also in adulteries, fornications, and the souls of men (chapter 18). Rome was even more a centre of corruption and decadence than of imperial glory and honour. Indeed, the honour and the glory of Rome were often inseparable from its corruption. As Rome was such a city then, so were Nineveh and Babylon before her, and so in degrees never precisely measurable are New York, Berlin, Tokyo, Delhi, Lagos, Rio de Janeiro, Nairobi, and a thousand other cities today.

The judgment of God will separate not only men who were good and men who were evil; it will also separate works that were good and works that were evil. 'Blessed are the dead who die in the Lord henceforth.' 'Blessed indeed,' says the Spirit, 'that they may rest from their labours, for their deeds (works) follow them!' (14:13). Inventions, paintings, sculptures, instruments, machines, tools, books, refined merchandise of gold, silver, wood, and precious stone, the loveliest fabrics of silk and costly textiles, the deep-toned drum, the melodious pipe, the far-seeing telescope—all, all shall be destroyed. Nothing shall survive the disintegration of all things physical. These all belong to the form of this world which is passing away (1 Corinthians 7:31). But the minds that conceived, planned, and devised these products of man's culture are imperishable. The kings of the earth— the kings of empires, the kings of the arts, the sciences, law, music, literature, worship—these kings will bring the honour and the glory of their diverse kingdoms into the new Jerusalem. Nothing thought and done by men which is true, honourable, just, pure, lovely, gracious, excellent, and worthy of praise (Philippians 4:8) shall be lost. The fruit of men's lives shall accompany their immortal spirits in their resurrection bodies to serve God in the new Jerusalem for ever.

This is not to suggest that the practitioners of culture have an automatic entrance into the new age. The new age is founded by, and is founded upon, the work of Christ. Only those who have been renewed by Him shall see the new Jerusalem. But this is a most significant fact. The Lord Jesus Christ is the one by whom God the Father created the world and He is the means for the redemption of men. All culture is the giving of shape and expression to fundamental laws that have from the beginning been imbedded in the created world. Not only to save the souls of men did Christ become incarnate and die for sin. He came no less to save the world (in Greek, the *cosmos*).

This is the deeper meaning of the oft-quoted John 3:16: 'God so loved the world that he gave his only Son, that whoever believes in him should not perish but have eternal life.' This life includes fellowship with and participation in the Logos who created the world (John 1:3, Colossians 1:15-17), in whom are hidden all treasures of wisdom and knowledge (Colossians 2:3).

The Church is the new humanity. She is rich and varied in her composition, as was the old humanity. The Church in Corinth, Paul said, did not count many who were powerful or of noble birth (1 Corinthians 1:26). But there were such men then, and later there were many. For centuries the light of culture and civilization in the West was kept alive by the Church. One great statesman, one great poet, philosopher, musician, scientist, historian, or artist is able to take up into himself a vast part of the cultural kingdom in which he reigns. When such a person belongs to Christ, as many do, he brings with him into the new Jerusalem all the riches which in life have been stored away in his mind and heart. It is in this way that the 'kings of the earth' shall bring the glory and the honour of many kingdoms into the holy city. The life to come shall build on the achievements of humanity throughout the long ages of our race. Those who have loved God shall enter into an inheritance rich beyond all description, and those who have not shall see the fruits of their labours given to those who have. Then shall be fulfilled the thought of Ecclesiastes beyond the farthest imagination of its writer: 'For to the man who pleases him God gives wisdom and knowledge and joy; but to the sinner he gives the work of gathering and heaping, only to give to one who pleases God' (2:26).

Revelation in its entirety has a very high Christology, fully supporting the New Testament teaching about the person of our Lord. But in distinction from the other books of the New Testament, Revelation is characterized by the fluid way in which it presents Him. We note that aspect of the book especially in its final chapter. In 22:8-13 one of the angels who had the seven bowls of the wrath of God speaks to John. In verse 9 he tells John not to worship him; he should worship God. In 22:12, however, he identifies himself with the Alpha and the Omega, who in 21:6 is very God. In 22:7 the angel also speaks as Christ in

'Behold, I am coming soon.' Chapter 22:16 distinguishes between 'I Jesus' and 'my angel'. At the same time the throne in heaven is occupied by 'God and the Lamb' in 22:1-3, but the Person worshipped in verse 3 is single: 'and his servants shall worship him; they shall see his face, and his name shall be on their foreheads'. We read, then, of identification of God and the Lamb, of distinction between them, and also of a fluidity between Christ and the angel through whom he speaks.

5   Concluding exhortations, 22:6-21

John's visions have run to their end. The 'things that must soon take place' have been shown. And He, whose angel revealed them, says, 'Surely I am coming soon'. There remain two closing exhortations. One is to obey the message of the book. The other is not to add to or to take away from it.

The message of Revelation is a message that must be obeyed. 'Blessed is he who keeps the words of the prophecy of this book'. But if it is to be obeyed, it must be taught and heard. Therefore, 'do not seal up the words of the prophecy of this book'. What is written in it will soon be fulfilled, for the time is near. It may well be that preaching will not alter the attitudes of men to the gospel. Indeed, the judgments of God lead them to curse Him the more. Therefore let the evildoer still do evil, let the filthy still be filthy. But likewise, let the righteous still be righteous, and the holy still be holy. Let the line between belief and unbelief, between the Church and the world, be ever so sharply drawn; but as for you, John, preach the Word of God. Do not be silent. The refusal of men to turn to God does not justify the silence of the Church. Soon He will come to reward the good and to judge the evil. Meanwhile, let the thirsty come and take of the water of life freely. As the Bride awaits the coming of the Bridegroom she says, 'Come'. And the Spirit that is within her says, 'Come'. Jesus replies, 'Surely, I am coming soon'. To these words John adds his own confession and prayer, 'Amen. Come, Lord Jesus'.

With this exclamation of hope, longing, and expectation, the book that speaks more than any other book in

Scripture about the suffering and the victory of the Church, comes to an end. Its last word is a benediction: 'The grace of the Lord Jesus be with all the saints, Amen'.

In the call to obey the teaching of his book, John speaks also a solemn warning. If anyone adds to the words of the prophecy of this book, God will add to him its plagues. And if anyone takes away from this prophecy, God will take away his share in the tree of life and in the holy city (21:18,19). This warning has not always been understood correctly. Some have seen in these words a threat that does not apply to the reading of any other book in the Bible. That is, however, a serious misreading of the passage. We have seen that Revelation teaches nothing that is not found in the Bible as a whole. It is only the apocalyptic form of the writing that distinguishes Revelation from the other books in Scripture. It is, therefore, difficult to see why the study of Revelation should lay upon its readers a greater responsibility than the reading or study of any other book in the Bible.

We have also seen that there are many different interpretations of Revelation. Obviously they cannot all be true. Does this mean that some interpreters who have wrongly understood the book or parts of it, but who have nevertheless been faithful and devout students of God's Word, have brought upon themselves the curse pronounced in verses 18 and 19? As Paul would say about some impossible thought, 'By no means!' The phrase, 'the words of the prophecy of this book', simply means the gospel, the message of salvation. The warning is no different than the one Paul speaks to the Galatians, 'there are some who trouble you and want to pervert the gospel of Christ. But even if we, or an angel from heaven, should preach to you a gospel contrary to that we preached to you, let him be accursed' (Galatians 1:7-8). Doubtless John had in mind individuals and groups like the Nicolaitans (Revelation 2:14,15), or such as he warned against in 1 John 2:18-22.

John's Revelation is pre-eminently a book for the Church, and God will honour testimony concerning it from all who seek responsibly to present its ancient message to contemporary man. Let our concern be to understand it and to obey it. 'He who has an ear, let him hear what the Spirit says to the churches.'

Meaning for today

Whoever has read Revelation with understanding finds at the end of it an unwritten but unavoidable question confronting him. It is: Do you believe what you have read? That is to say: Do you believe that the Church stands at the centre of a great struggle between the powers of light and the powers of darkness? Do you believe that Jesus Christ through His life, death, and resurrection is already now the Victor in that struggle? Do you believe that God will one day reveal the new heavens and the new earth as the fruit of Christ's victory? Do you believe that the redeemed Church will live in unbroken fellowship with God and with His Christ in that new creation?

If such questions are answered with a genuine 'Yes', then by that fact our lives are controlled by a powerful hope. Our final *Meaning for Today* may therefore appropriately draw on the truth that John expressed in his first epistle:

> And every one who thus hopes in him purifies himself as he is pure. (3:3)

Hope is a powerful activity of the human spirit. Hope is goodness, hope is achievement, hope is satisfaction, hope is joy—but in the form of desire and expectation. Hope drives one on to turn expectation into possession, anticipation into realization. Like the need for food, work, rest, and fellowship, hope is rooted in man's very nature. Therefore the saying, 'Hope springs eternal in the human breast', speaks a truth that men live by. When hope fades and dies in the heart of a man, the body soon pines away and dies with it. Terrible are the words which a poet in his vision saw written above the gates of hell: 'All hope abandon, ye who enter here.'

However powerful the human need for hope is, it is, nevertheless, no more than desire, expectation, longing. It never contains certainty. There is no guarantee that it will become a reality. For this reason it is necessary to understand what the New Testament means by hope. It is not hope in the dictionary sense of the word. It is not simply a wish, a deep desire, a longing, an expectation that may or may not be fulfilled. The Christian hope, the hope that is the fruit of faith in Christ, is a present reality. It is a present certainty. It is here and now fact. When we hope that it will rain tomorrow, it is not in fact raining today.

But when we hope in life everlasting, then that hope is today a great reality. He that believes in Christ *has* eternal life. The hope of life everlasting is not so much an expectation as an awaiting of the full manifestation of what we already have. Paul compared the eternal life we have now and the eternal life that we wait for with the first-fruits of the harvest and the full harvest itself. All the new life that we have in Christ, the new relationships to God, to our neighbour, and to the world around us, and not least the new relationship to ourselves, exist now as incomplete but they exist in Christ in their fulness.

We do not know what the form or quality will be of the new heavens and the new earth, or of the new Jerusalem within that new creation. But we know it will be wonderful. Already God has revealed through his Spirit 'what no eye has seen, nor ear heard, nor the heart of man conceived, what God has prepared for those who love him' (1 Corinthians 2:9,10). Therefore John writes, 'Beloved, we are God's children now; it does not yet appear what we shall be, but we know that when he appears we shall be like him, for we shall see him as he is. And everyone who thus hopes in him purifies himself as he is pure' (1 John 3:2,3).

This act of self-purification is a powerful witness to the presence in us of the new life that Christ has brought. John does not say that everyone who hopes in Christ ought to purify himself, or should purify himself, or consider it is his duty to purify himself. He says that he *does in fact* now purify himself. The new life cannot sin. The new life rejects it. The new life in Christ can only do good. The sin we still commit flows from our old nature, not from the new. Therefore the man who hopes in Christ necessarily does good. It is the only activity of which that life is capable. The life of Christian obedience is, therefore, a great testimony to the validity of the Christian hope that we have and to the reality of the new life out of which it flows.

If our citizenship is in heaven (Philippians 3:20), then we are now members and citizens of the new Jerusalem. Those who live away from their homeland have the desire to live in the foreign land in such a way as shall bring credit on the land of their birth and citizenship. The vision of the new heavens and the new earth in which the new

Jerusalem stands must lead us to ask whether we reveal ourselves to be the kind of men and women that we profess to be. For we are called not to a dead hope, but to a *living* hope (1 Peter 1:2-5).

In his noted devotional book, *The Imitation of Christ,* Thomas à Kempis writes,

> A certain man, being in anxiety, often wavered between fear and hope, and once, being oppressed with grief, humbly prostrated himself in church before the altar in prayer, and meditated within himself, saying, 'Oh! if I knew that I should still persevere.'
>
> And presently he heard within him an answer from God, 'And if you knew, what would you do? Do now what you would do then, and you will be very secure.'
>
> And forthwith, being comforted and strengthened, he committed himself wholly to the will of God, and that anxious fluctuation ceased. (Book 1, Ch. 25)

Jesus said, 'If you love me, keep my commandments'. Even so, come, Lord Jesus.

Typesetting by Nuprint Services Limited, Harpenden, Hertfordshire, U.K.